T0332296

# Write Now!

This book will make you an influential business writer – the one who cuts through the noise and changes what your readers think, feel and do.

Business writing often seems frightening, and seriously great writing is rare in the workplace. If writing has been taught at all, it's through managers covering errors with red ink or online trolls complaining about grammar. This book offers a kinder, gentler and funnier way to improve your writing, from an author who's taught around the world and is encouraging, original, fun and always supportive. Whether you read parts in sequence or jump to the topics that most interest you, with this hands-on guide at your side, you will:

- Understand what readers want from writers
- Write with confidence and style
- Structure and plan your writing
- Overcome writer's block
- Get more readers

Anyone who has to write for business – to convince, to break down barriers and simply to express themselves well – will welcome the road-tested tips and techniques in this light-hearted and practical guide.

**Andreas Loizou** teaches business writing and storytelling around the world. His clients include leading global banks, think tanks and consultancies. Andreas has a Master of Studies in English from Cambridge. He started his career with PWC, worked as an investment analyst at Goldman Sachs and was director of training at Financial Times Knowledge. His books *The Devil's Deal* and *The Story Is Everything* have been translated into over 20 languages. Andreas also founded the world-famous Margate Bookie writing festival.

# Write Now!

## How to Influence and Connect with your Business Writing

**Andreas Loizou**

Routledge
Taylor & Francis Group

NEW YORK AND LONDON

Designed cover image: Getty

First published 2025
by Routledge
605 Third Avenue, New York, NY 10158

and by Routledge
4 Park Square, Milton Park, Abingdon, Oxon, OX14 4RN

*Routledge is an imprint of the Taylor & Francis Group, an informa business*

© 2025 Andreas Loizou

ISBN: 978-1-032-84497-8 (hbk)
ISBN: 978-1-032-84155-7 (pbk)
ISBN: 978-1-003-51352-0 (ebk)

DOI: 10.4324/9781003513520

Typeset in Sabon
by Apex CoVantage, LLC

To Karen Benn, with love and gratitude.

# Contents

# Acknowledgments

Grateful thanks to all those who helped with *Write Now!*

Richard Bastin, Ouida Taaffe, John Tague, Peter Cross, Lesley Henderson, Meredith Norwich, Bethany Nelson, Adhilakshmi Parasuraman and everyone at Team Bookie.

Photos by Benjamin Bowles, mosaic by Jas Selman.

Right, time to write the next one…

# Part 1

# Clarity

## Why Everyone Loves Great Writing

# Chapter 1

# Inside a reader's mind

I see the person I'm talking to as I write.

I use *talking to* deliberately. I want you to feel we are in a conversation, even if I can't hear your side of the story.

The person I see in my mind's eye is intelligent but isn't an expert in business writing. You have high standards and want to make an impact. You're friendly and supportive, but you're pushed for time. The dull words that fill our lives – *silo, paradigm shift,* anything ending in *centric* – turn you off.

You deserve 'real' words rather than coma-inducing abstractions. Let's kick out *results-orientated* and *synergistic* and let in words that evoke the senses.

I imagine you reading this on holiday on a beautiful Greek Island, all deep blue seas and massive skies. You push open the door to a small café down by the harbour, hear the hum of fans, feel a cooling breeze on your face. You breathe in freshly ground coffee and sweet pastries covered in honey and almonds.

Even before you take your first bite of filo pastry, your mouth is watering and your whole body is expectant. Reading this has made your mouth water, hasn't it? Writing that connects changes what a reader feels, thinks and does.

An email pings up on your screen. It's from the office. *Ongoing implementations of catering facilities solutions.* A single tear falls from your eye as you come to a realisation.

We can do better than this.

## Write with the reader in mind

Here's a useful paradox about writing. The more you focus on a single reader, the more your writing connects with many different people.

Successful influencers convince millions of viewers and listeners that they are talking only to them. They visualise a single person – it could be a woman

DOI: 10.4324/9781003513520-2

stuck in traffic on the way home or a schoolboy doing his homework. The more specific the visualisation – what colour is her car? What is the exam he's cramming for? – the more comfortable they are speaking to them.

It's all about *humanisation* (I've checked, and that is a word). Business people often believe that their target audience is everyone, and as a consequence, they see no-one as they write. That's the mindset that produces flabby, bland writing that changes absolutely no-one.

The most dehumanised writers are the fake experts. The internet is overrun with phonies, and the giveaway is how they condescend to their readers. While true experts prefer to explain and inspire, these people talk down to us. Their language choice betrays them. Multisyllabic words, unexplained jargon terms, deliberately complex phrases when simpler alternatives exist. Instead of the fastest and freshest way to get their ideas across, they choose ponderous sentence structures and a pontificating tone of voice.

Don't be the person who writes *at this current moment of time* instead of *now*.

## Why you are buying this book

Is that a jolt of scepticism flashing across your face? Perhaps you need some more convincing.

Good writing – seriously great writing – is rare in the workplace. I'm not claiming that great business writing skills lead to fame, fortune and true love. But it's worth a try, yep?

We all think we can write, because we can put together a shopping list without too much difficulty. But most of us get anxious and blocked when writing at work because no-one has ever taught us the best ways to spread our message. If we've learned at all, it's through managers covering our errors with red ink or online trolls publicly shaming our grammar. A well-meaning colleague may edit us in Word, and all we see is blocks of angry red crossing-outs.

There is a kinder, gentler, funnier way to improve your writing. And you're reading it now.

## When benefits change emotions

The classic advice from advertisers is to sell benefits, rather than features. So you should stress *you'll love the music as you drive to work* rather than *these speakers come with 4 Way 4 Inch Replacement Neodymium Magnet Bonding*, unless your audience is very technical.

It's far easier to sell a book (or just about everything) if the customer understands how it will benefit them. Too many people concentrate on the features of what they've produced. That's like me trying to interest you in

*Write Now!* by talking about how nice the paper is, or mentioning that the cover is quite shiny. These features are undeniably true, and they may be enough to convince you to click buy on Amazon, but most of us need more convincing reasons to buy. There's an emotional level deeper than benefits which you can reach with your writing.

Back to you. I want to tell you about four benefits you'll gain by reading this book. My focus is on the positive emotions you'll feel.

### 1. Success

You're writing because you have objectives to fulfil. Persuasive, clear writing helps you achieve them. Your new writing skills can inspire millions, or stop the new intern from photocopying their private parts. Either way, your writing has changed the reader.

### 2. Time

Forget all those hours you spent procrastinating, moving commas and deleting what you've just written. You'll write in a way that saves you hours and hours on every project. You're not just saving your own time – readers love writing they can understand immediately.

### 3. Admiration

We all like people who can express themselves well. Good writing gets you noticed, for all the right reasons. A lot of business writing is cold, dry and abstract. It's rare for it to connect with humans, so any writer who shows empathy and charisma will be worshipped.

### 4. Status

Good writers influence what we think, feel and do. They tend to be the people we follow. The extra work you put in now will make you stand out from the crowd.

What does all this positivity get you? This book is ultimately about increasing your happiness. Being more successful, having more time, being admired and enjoying higher status are all great things. But being happy in what you do? That's the best feeling in the working world.

### This books splits into five parts

You can read the chapters in sequence or jump around to the topics that most interest you. There are some short exercises I really hope you do, as well as *Where to Now* suggestions to follow up.

Part 1 is all about Great Writing. You'll learn how to make people select you in a world where they're bombarded by other choices. Part 2 takes you through the Nuts and Bolts of Writing, all the way from the overall structure of your masterpiece to the precise placing of a comma. Part 3 turns you from a good writer into a Writer of Influence. It's full of ways to attract and keep followers.

In Part 4, we'll look at Charisma, that elusive element that makes readers love you. I'm a big believer in learning from people who are much smarter than me, so this part has examples from all around the world. And with Part 5, we finish off with ways you can polish your writing until it shines.

### Write Now!

| Why Everyone Loves Great Writing | The Nuts and Bolts of Writing | How to Be a Writer of Influence | Charisma Connects with the Reader | Polish Makes Your Diamond Shine |
|---|---|---|---|---|
| Why Readers Choose You | Structure and Planning | Persuasion and Influence | Rapport and Connection | Editing, Revising, Proofing |
| The Emotions of Writing | Intros, Paragraphs, Sentences | Style and Voice | The Quest for Clarity | Summaries, Design and Visuals |
| How People Read | Words, Grammar, Punctuation | Messages with Impact | Business Storytelling | Readability |

### Where to now?

Later on I'll give you suggestions, so you can jump around the chapters. But for now, I'm going to be super conventional and ask you to dive straight into Chapter 2.

# Chapter 2

# What do you want from your writing?

I've taught writing all over the world to many different types of people – NGO workers from Madagascar, architects in Rome, security chiefs in the shadow of a heavily guarded oil terminal jutting into the Thames. People are remarkably similar in what they want their writing to be.

*Hit List* – clear, concise, accurate, stylish, human, relevant, popular with readers

They're also very clear about what they want to avoid.

*Shit List* – boring, repetitive, dull, muddled, too long, corporate, unclear

All of my lovely students want to influence how their readers think, feel and act. They want to feel confident and in control as they write and proud of what they publish. They like the sensation of having planned their work. They hate being ignored because their work is too late or unwanted, or so badly written that people swear out loud when they open their email.

I reckon all of this applies to you as well. (That's pretty much why you bought this book, right?) Let's see how we make all these good things happen.

This chapter couldn't be further away from a list of writing rules. It's much more about being aware of your reasons for writing.

## Check your motivations

There are two sources of motivation for writers.

*Intrinsic motivation* comes from personal desire. You draw cartoons because it's fun; you study fine art because you find the subject interesting. When you write with intrinsic motivation, you're primarily writing for yourself.

*Extrinsic motivation* comes from other people and the wider world. You draw cartoons because you can sell them for 50 dollars a pop; you study fine art because your parents will buy you a gallery when you finish your degree.

DOI: 10.4324/9781003513520-3

Intrinsic motivation trumps extrinsic every time. Feeling happy about your writing is a powerful motivator. You don't need financial rewards if the process of writing is enjoyable. It's something you look forward to, and that's enough to keep you going.

But if your writing is tough and tricky and boring and stressful (i.e., you're writing at work) then you need the compensation of external motivation to keep your nose to the grindstone. The problem is that external rewards – cash, basically – suffer from diminishing returns. If you're doing any task just for money, over time you will need more and more money to keep you motivated.

It's the difference between going on a romantic weekend and giving your lover a bottle of expensive wine, or handing them over a roll of banknotes equal to the value of that bottle. The cash value may be exactly the same, but the message you send about motivation will be very, very different.

A word in your ear. Sometimes the line between intrinsic and extrinsic motivation isn't as clear as the psychologists would have us believe. It's tempting to see intrinsic and extrinsic motivations as different and even opposed. But I encourage you to look for the links. For most of you, writing is part of your job, so you are doing it for money. Don't see this as a bad thing! But look for the intrinsic motivation that will keep your motor spinning. What is it about the task that makes you happy, stretches you, keeps you growing? It's the intrinsic motivation that will keep you writing, long after your pleas for more money have faded into silence.

## Three mindsets to boost your intrinsic motivation

I have good news to share with you. Intrinsic motivation – which will make you more determined, happier and simply *better* as a writer – can be grown. There are three ways to make this happen.

## Autonomy

We're more motivated when we feel we have control over what we do. You might not have control over the objective of a task (the reason why it's been commissioned) but you do have control over how you present it (the style and spirit with which you write it). Show people you're a good writer whose ideas are worth reading. Put your case forward, be prepared to disagree with comments when it's necessary. Own it.

## Competence

Focus on what you're learning, rather than just nailing an item on your To Do list. You're not churning out junk emails, but learning how to craft killer sentences that open the hearts, minds and wallets of resistant readers. This mindset will keep you searching for higher degrees of challenge, and that's going to keep you moving forward as an individual.

## Relatedness

Understand how your writing fits into a bigger cause. Your sceptical mind might tell you that those Instagram posts about heroin use are a waste of time, so remind yourself that you're campaigning for a change in how people view drug abuse. The writing reflects what's important to you; I'm not going to throw about words like *values, beliefs* and *passions* here, but you get the picture.

Stop reading for 30 seconds and think about the next thing you're going to write. What are your motivations, intrinsic and extrinsic, for writing it? Get some paper and jot down these motivations. Notice how stating your motivations makes you more enthusiastic.

## Check your emotions

I want to tell you about the Fear Index before you start your next project. It measures how afraid you are of writing. It ignores what's making you nervous – fear of criticism, imposter syndrome, a deep-rooted hatred of your boss – and instead quantifies your worries with a number. It's totally subjective, so you can't get it wrong.

Think about the next thing you need to write. Where do you put yourself on the scale?

| 1 | 2 | 3 | 4 | 5 | 6 | 7 | 8 | 9 | 10 |
|---|---|---|---|---|---|---|---|---|---|
| Great | Easy like Sunday morning | No Prob | OK | Ok-ish | Hmmm . . . | Nervy | Afraid | Shaky | Night-mares |

Some people are blessed with amazing levels of self-confidence. They'll be at 1, 2 or 3 whatever writing task is in front of them. But most people are nervy about writing. A manageable feeling of trepidation can be good because it's proof you care about what you're doing. But if you're at 8, 9 or 10, your anxiety will create a barrier between you and your writing.

The Fear Index isn't a cure for lack of talent, poor planning, emotional blocks or procrastination. But it does make you more conscious of your nerves. Everything that follows in this chapter – indeed, pretty much everything that's coming up in this entire book – is about making you more confident with your writing and reducing that fear.

## How does writing happen?

We're all looking for that secret that unlocks writing. Perhaps there's a lucky pen that will make your first drafts flow, or a mysterious app that turns your ill-considered ramblings into highly polished prose. You'll be a winner, if only you could buy that magic mug or learn the special way writers cross their legs under the desk.

It's nothing like that. It doesn't matter if you are a start-up entrepreneur, the CEO of a charity or the custodian of a portfolio worth billions. Nor does it matter if you're writing a 400-page academic tome or a 250-word blog. The really successful writers I work with share a very similar approach. They split their production[1] into three parts – thinking, writing and revising.

### Thinking

The thoughts in your mind represent who you are and what you believe at this very short and specific moment in time. Some people's thoughts change constantly and dramatically; other people never change their mind at all.

We often use phrases like *the thoughts going round my head* or *the ideas rambling around my brain*. This language suggests that our thoughts are wild and unstructured and that they would benefit from some corralling. We can take control of our ideas by writing them down.

### Writing

Writing unclogs the brain. If you've got a writing job to do, blast out a first version as quickly as you can. It doesn't matter if it's full of crossings out and notes to yourself like *find out more* or *wtf did he mean when he said that?* The worst thing you write will still be much better than a blank screen.

Getting words down means you won't get tripped up by your fears. Writing always leads to more writing. Set your target – 400 words, 20 minutes – get focused and go for it.

### Revision

The best writers are constantly revising, moving words and paragraphs around. This is distinct from editing (which we look at in Chapter 17) because it happens while you're still in the first draft.

In my own writing, I am constantly on the lookout for:

*Areas of confusion.* They tell me my thoughts aren't clear or the order of my argument is wrong.

*Lack of focus.* I've got distracted, so my writing is repetitious or verbose. This always happens when I'm tired.

*Too much going on.* I've got too many ideas to jam into a limited word count. I ask myself what is the 10% of the text that's absolutely essential and what are the main points that would go into an executive summary? If these are clear, I'm golden.

## What Marcus Aurelius tells us about thinking and writing

Most of us first met Marcus Aurelius in *Gladiator*. Rome's great philosopher-emperor, played with panache by Richard Harris, has to choose a successor. His son, the loathsome and narcissistic Commodus, is furious because his father prefers Maximus, the empire's leading general. In the movie, Commodus, clearly not a man to let familial bonds stand in his way, kills his father and forces Maximus into exile.

Marcus Aurelius only gets a five-minute cameo on screen. A shame for us writers, because here was a man who managed to write every day, despite leading his empire in battle after battle across Europe.

Marcus Aurelius' most famous book, *Meditations*, wasn't planned as a book at all. His journaling was a way to clear his mind. If he could keep his journal after a hard day of slaughter and destruction, surely you can find ten minutes to get that last email done?

Here are four tips that I've distilled from his writing. Maybe, just maybe, you'll find perspective in what he had to say two millennia before.

### We can't control events, but we can control our thoughts and emotions about these events

We all get blocked and distracted, irritated and annoyed. But what's important is how you react to these feelings, rather than the feelings themselves. Accept them as a natural part of writing, rather than a personal attack from the Muses, and you'll be much happier and productive. Calm the monkey mind, and then get focused.

### Writing declutters your thoughts by creating space in your brain

In an age where authors have Twitter profiles years before they even have a publishing deal, it seems odd to write just for ourselves. I'm always stressing how important it is to consider our audience, but this is an area where I want you to just write for you. I don't like the phrase *mind dump*, but there is value in getting all the old stuff down on paper. If not, how are you going to create space to allow the new thoughts in?

I started journaling in the first week of the first lockdown, and I'm never going to stop. It takes ten minutes at an absolute max and I find it makes writing much easier. I start by listing five things from yesterday that put me in a good mood. Of course, I wish this was stuff like *yet another Oscar nomination* or *signed multi-million pound deal for next book* but *went for coffee with Madame Khan* is just as effective in boosting my mood.

Then I list three things I want to achieve during the day. This is more about *finish first draft of* Chapter 2 rather than *pick up curtains from dry cleaners*. I see this as a To Be list, rather than a To Do list, because how we spend our days is how we spend our lives.

I might also jot down some random notes about books I'm reading or why I liked an article in the *FT*, but now I'm ready. Happy state established, mind cleared, objectives set, eager to write.

### Good writers learn from great writers

Deep reading improves the mind. Marcus Aurelius put it better, of course, when he advised, 'read with diligence. Do not rest satisfied with a light and superficial knowledge'.

If you read with care and attention, you'll learn how great writers change you. And if you re-read your favourites, the lessons will stick with you for ever.

### Getting your ideas in order always leads to new ideas

Imposing order on your thoughts is an odd task. You have loads of stuff, good and bad, swirling around your head. I sometimes suffer from two completely contradictory fears while I'm writing.

1. I will never have another idea in my life.
2. I will never control all the ideas I have.

Accept this swing between famine and feast as part of the normal rhythm of planning. Thoughts fly around, change direction, look for a flock to join. Let them come together.

Let's take a six-minute break and do something different. I want you to try this game with me. It's simple and fun and tells us a lot about how we think.

Put a pen on your desk and stare at it for one minute. Don't let your eyes wander. Then set a timer, giving yourself three minutes to write down as many uses as you can imagine for the pen. You can use it for writing, for scratching your back, for propping up your computer. You'll run out of ideas round about two minutes and 20 seconds, if not before.

Now find a second object – I'm using an old school bank card – and look around the room and out of the window and across the street for a minute. What uses can you imagine for the card? It can jam open a broken window, keep a cup from staining a café's pristine white tablecloth, level up the same café's slightly wonky table, cut flowers, cut toast, spring open a door, trim herbs, be a temporary bookmark, clean your nails, part your hair and so many other things that you might even find that three minutes isn't enough for all you've invented.

What do we learn? Our ideas flow naturally and easily when our mind is open to new influences. Staring out of the window may not be the problem that your teachers always said it was. Open you mind, and the ideas will come to you.

## Where to now?

Chapter 4 – look at how the environment you create, and the messages you send yourself, can give you a jolt of positivity

Chapter 5 – consider Bottom-Up Thinking and Top-Down Communication. Have you got enough of both in your writing process?

Chapter 12 – still feeling anxious? Learn how the six bricks boost your confidence.

## Note

1 I've deliberately chosen this word, with its echoes of factories and processes and ordered design. Business writing is rarely the place for *I wandered lonely as a cloud* type of musing.

Chapter 3

# How to make readers choose you

## F Me

Online readers are pushed for time and very harsh. The stats are terrifying. Research suggests less than 16% of the words in a business post get read, and only one in five people who reach the bottom of the screen are tempted to click on the down arrow and read a second page. Distracted by a million alternatives, even your most faithful readers don't stick around.

Some of you will mutter about the good old days when we had more time to read and less demands on our attention. The truth is that readers have always skimmed books and articles. Indeed, many of us only passed exams because we knew what to study and what to jettison. The difference today is that all of us skim for pretty much most of the time. What's worrying is that our offline reading is, every day and in every way, becoming more and more and more and more like our online scanning. (I've made this sentence deliberately long and repetitious. You skimmed it, didn't you?)

## How we read online

You might think that brains are slowing down, but have you ever noticed just how quick our eyes are becoming? We zap through pages at an incredible speed, gleaning what we need as rapidly as possible. And we do this in ways that are entirely predictable.

Our eyes make an F shape when we're reading online.

DOI: 10.4324/9781003513520-4

Eyes travel across first headline

First sentence probably gets read

Looking for lists

Looking for bullets

Scan half of subheading

Words of interest

No focus

Bored

Next!

Readers start at the top left. Then their eyes move horizontally along the headline. Some read the whole headline, but most usually don't. If they do get as far as your second paragraph, it's very unlikely that will reach its final sentence.

Then they scan down the left-hand side. Their eyes dart around looking for clues about the content – numbered lists, short bullet points, subtitles in bold. Readers scan subheadings, but usually just the first three or four words.

Readers are desperate for anything that piques their interest. It could be a word or phrase that's important to them now – *bond yield, Harry Potter, conifers*. Maybe a picture, maybe a graph. The farther down they go, the less they find of interest. Their focus fizzles out round about the fourth paragraph.

Now we know what gets looked at, let's think about what gets missed. Anything on the right-hand side of the page will get less traction. Long headlines don't get read, long paragraphs are ignored, not even your biggest fan will get to the bottom of your piece. What do we do? Face facts, we're not going to be able to change how humankind chooses to read. We have to accept that skimming is a fact of a writer's life and, rather than getting all hissy and throwing our quills away in disgust, we must change to grab readers' attention. Every reader is busy and drowning in choices. The onus is on you to change how you write – and how you present your writing – to make them pick you.

## How can you benefit from scanning and skimming?

The phrase *establish your visual hierarchy* sounds like the sort of guff an advertising exec would pronounce to a client after their third Macha Martini. But ignore their advice at your peril. Now you know how readers scan, it's relatively easy to keep them engaged with these nine easy tips.

1. Get you main message across first.[1] If they read and remember only this, your job as a writer has been done. This means putting most of your writing and editing time into the headline and the first sentences.
2. Your most expensive visual estate resides top left. This is usually the best place to have your call to action, your discount code, your sign up button. Don't have them at the bottom of the page, which is a very different neighbourhood.
3. Start lower paragraphs with short sentences, key words and highlighted text. Avoid unneeded beginnings like *in my opinion* and *it is a truth universally considered*. They just lose you readers in the unforgiving online world.
4. Give reasons to move down the left-hand side of the page. Put key words in bold and italic (but be aware of the Just Noticeable Difference rule we look at in Chapter 8). Use numbered lists (like I'm doing here) rather than bullet points.
5. Blank space gets the eye moving. This is counterintuitive, but white space appeals to the reader. It's a bit like the scene in a crime novel where the cop is interviewing the criminal. Lots of short, sharp sentences move the reader rapidly through the text.
6. It doesn't work for everyone. Some people scan in an inverted L pattern; some are partial to E's. And be mindful that not every reader has grown up reading from left to right.
7. Big solid blocks of text are unappealing. People will skim a 12-line paragraph very quickly, so consider cutting it into three blocks of four lines each.
8. Headers and subheadings – break up the text so a reader's eyes can rest. And make sure your headings contain your key words.
9. Simple formatting techniques – **bold**, for example – grab the eye.

## Where to now?

Chapter 6 – raise your paragraph game. Put most of your effort into the topic sentence rather than the supporting sentences. This is what the habitual skimmer will read.

Chapter 19 – learn how the philosophy of JND (the *just noticeable difference*) will get you eyeballs.

Try this – take a visit to a bookshop and be conscious of how the books are displayed. Notice how your eyes are immediately drawn to the bestsellers that lie flat on a table when you come in. And why are reference books at the back of the shop or even downstairs? What is about the design and layout of the shop that influences what you buy?

## Note

1  This won't be the last time I mention this point.

# Chapter 4

# Creating the best environment and mindset for writing

How we write is immensely personal. We all operate at different levels of confidence, and we all have different reasons to feel good or bad about our next writing task. None of us has enough time to accomplish our objectives, and most of us will be distracted by thoughts about work (can I make the marketing meeting?) or life (can I get my daughter to her volleyball match on time?) as we wrestle with our words.

We can't ignore these factors, but we can handle them in smart ways. I'm wary of the one-size-fits-all approach when offering advice on the emotions of writing, but I've noticed two areas – your writing conditions and the messages you send yourself – that most writers can improve.

## Time, space and noise

Or, to be more accurate, this is about your reaction to these external influences. You need to work this out, or writing will always feel uncomfortable.

Many of us prefer to write early. But some of us are nightbirds, especially when a deadline is close. None of us writes well in the 90 minutes after lunch, when we're sleepy and energy moves down from our brain into our tummy.

You might believe writing is a rather private activity, and so you burrow down into your own space. Others – invariably the most extrovert of our colleagues – need an audience. They like to tell people what they're working on and they draw energy from a buzzy office.

We're all affected by noise. I play music, and others slip on headphones that play white noise or cancel out all the sounds around them. Some people want cathedral-like silence and tut when anyone taps too loudly on their keyboard.

You need to control these *environmental factors*. I know it's sometime hard to control your writing space, whether you're in an office or at home, but your productivity and personal happiness will soar with even just minor changes.

DOI: 10.4324/9781003513520-5

## Improve your writing environment with this quick task

I want you to think about Time, Space and Noise. List what works for you and what doesn't. Just two minutes on this will make you more productive and – quite possibly – much happier.

|  | What Works for You | What Doesn't Work for You |
|---|---|---|
| Time |  |  |
| Space |  |  |
| Noise |  |  |

Figure 4.1 Create your ideal writing environment with time, space and noise

## Self-messages

There's a lot going on between our ears as we write. Writing – especially when you're struggling with those first vital words – can make your confidence evaporate. I'm aware that telling people to be confident when they're feeling emotionally shaky is as irritating and as useless as a nurse ordering you to relax just before she shoves a syringe into your arm. But I do think it's worth checking if your mindset is working against you. Here are three mini-mantras that just might stop the self-sabotage.

*Accept Imperfection.* You can make your writing better, but you can never make it perfect. And nor should you. Do you really think spending another day re-drafting that email about expense claims is the best use of your time? Let it go, as the princesses sing in *Frozen.*

*Embrace the Audience.* Thinking more about your readers will increase your desire to write to them. Remind yourself that the vast majority of people in the world want you to succeed, so tell your inner critic to shut up because you have a message to spread.

*Expect Rejection.* Not everyone wants to hear from you. Sometimes a negative response has nothing to do with you or your writing. Your reader may be having a bad day. Or a bad life. Cut yourself some slack, because not every negative reaction is your fault.

Poor environmental factors and negative self-messaging can sometimes lead to you feeling blocked. If you're feeling stale and bored, you're not going to produce writing of worth. It's better to change your environment and your mental state, rather than struggling through brain fog.

My first recommendation is to *rest*. Tired writers produce exhausted writing. Take a nap, clear you mind with meditation or just do nothing for 20 minutes. My second tip is *get up and move*. Go for a stomp around your local park or, if you're working at home, now's the time to watch that 10-minute beginner's guide to salsa on YouTube. A little bit of shake and shimmy will get your endorphins boogying around your body, and that's going to make you a better writer. Exercise lifts the spirits and disconnects the irritating monkey mind. When you return to your writing, you'll feel energised and eager. Promise.

## The body of a writer

There's a (surprisingly) powerful link between how you sit and how you write. Let me explain as we walk around Broadstairs, a small seaside town five miles from where I grew up. Charles Dickens took his holidays in Broadstairs and the town works its Dickens connections hard. You can drink in the Charles Dickens pub, eat in the Charles Dickens curry house and attend the Charles Dickens school, though hopefully not on the same day. You can saunter to Bleak House and you can order a pint of Betsey Trotwood in a pub that was once called the Barnaby Rudge, and then stroll up to Bleak House. Sadly, the newsagents isn't called the Pickwick Papers and no-one has yet opened a Mexican restaurant called *Little Dorritos*.

The Dickens House Museum overlooks beautiful Viking Bay. Its exhibits – some letters written by Dickens, some prints by his book illustrator – aren't extensive. But the display of Victorian furniture gives me an idea.

Let me explain something about body language. I had always believed that body language *reflects* a person's mental state. If you're frightened, you'll clench in your stomach, and if you're nervous, you clasp your hands tightly across your chest. So far, so predictable. But what I later learned was that body language can also *create* our mental state. If we walk tall, with our chest open and shoulders back, we immediately feel more confident.

Look around you and find someone who is *slumping* at their desk. Copy how their body sags, and notice how their head seems too heavy for their neck to hold up. Perhaps you can feel your eyelids fluttering to a close, because you are as lethargic and lacking in energy as they are, and maybe no-one will spot if you have five minutes of shut-eye . . .

Hardly the ideal state for productivity, is it? But it's a common posture for someone who's been sat at their desk too long.

The table and chair that Dickens used for writing aren't particularly comfortable. They make you want to sit up straight. Dickens was prolific (he wrote 14 novels, dying during the 15th) and knew that some chairs are for work, and others for relaxing. There's a chaise longue where you can imagine him resting after a long, hard morning of writing and an agreeably heavy lunch in the *Grape Expectations*. One of the paradoxes of productive people is that they certainly know how to relax.

Now look around for someone who seems ready for action. They'll almost certainly be striding around, leaning forward, eager to connect. I now imagine Dickens at the museum's lectern, reading aloud as he stands up to edit.

The chair, the lectern and the chaise longue. Think of them as the three mental states you enter when you're writing, revising and resting. Being aware of them will make you more productive *and* more relaxed. How we position our bodies has a huge impact on our writing success. Change your body language, and magic will happen.

## Three ways to change your body language for writing

These changes in posture will be reflected in writing that's more grabby and more authoritative. Words on paper affect readers on a cognitive level, but here's the weird thing. We are also communicating our physical state to the reader.

Smile – you've just won the lottery, finally kissed your dream date, scored the last minute winner and grabbed the modelling contract. All on the same day! Notice how much more active and alive you feel just by imagining these successes.

Stretch – get up and inhale as much new air as you can. That's right – mouth open, arms outstretched, eyes wide, lungs full. Feel the new writing energy in your veins.

Stand to attention – feet wide, shoulders broad, chin up. You are the admiral surveying the fleet. Immediately you're ready for the fight.

## Plan it all

The longer the project, the greater the positive impact of planning. I always draw up a list of the main points I need to cover, even if I'm just writing a three paragraph email. For longer pieces, I use any method I can find to help me project manage my ideas. I've never found the perfect software, and probably never will, but over the years I've used Notify, Scrivener, Excel, Slack, Teams and so many others. It's all personal, so find a way that suits you and keep in mind that different approaches work for different writing tasks.

I started planning *Write Now!* with a hand-drawn mindmap. (It was originally going to be called *Message*, but everything is changeable.) I keep my mindmaps as simple as I can. I can't draw, so there's no point me adding

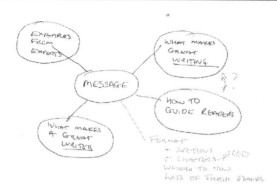

*Figure 4.2 The best mindmaps always start scruffy*

graphics, and my daughter steals my stationery so it's a miracle if I can find different coloured pens to jazz things up.

The first mindmap only took up half a page of A4. The black boxes represent content areas, the arrows and question mark show where I had a doubt about section order.

This first, tiny mindmap grew quickly. I kept it unfolded on my desk so I didn't have to hunt for it every time I thought of a great example or a reference to follow up. I scribbled down ideas and glued new pages to it as it expanded. It ended up covered with post it notes, web addresses, inspiring books and 4 am scrawls I couldn't decipher in the morning. As soon as it was too big for the table – say about six pages in total – I fired up the mindmapping software.

Then I concentrated on putting some order on all these random thoughts. I searched for connections, deleted repetitions, added areas to research. A picture's worth a thousand words, and all that, so here's how part two of the book looked at this stage.

Take a look at the branch called *Summary Heaven*. It doesn't matter that I can only remember two of the four steps to writing a summary or that I have forgotten what I meant when I wrote *BITLY*. A mindmap's job is to give you the shape of a book, even if you don't know all the details.

It's only now that I start to write. I might produce an entire chapter in one sitting, or take a day to write 500 words. What matters to me is that my writing has a purpose. I know exactly where my words fit in the book before I've begun the sentence.

## Planning defeats fear every time

Just because you've got a plan, it doesn't mean that you have to follow it. The very process of writing will create new ideas. You may find better ways

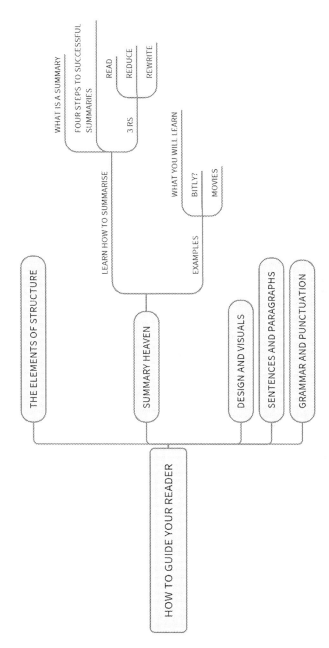

*Figure 4.3 Mindmaps need to change and grow*

to structure your report as you become more familiar with the content. Some areas will strike you as vital, so what was a footnote two weeks ago may now be an entire chapter. You may discover that certain topics are less relevant than you originally thought.

## A set format helps you plan

I'm lucky because my editor, Meredith, agreed on a structure for the book very early. We wanted five sections, split into four chapters, with between 1,600 and 1,800 words in each chapter. So I knew the final book had to be between 32,000 and 36,000 words.

Here's the odd thing. Having these constrictions made it much *easier* for me to plan. And that planning, as a consequence, made it much easier for me to write.

If you're commissioned to write a report, and the client doesn't tell you how long they want it to be, ask them. If they don't help you, then place restrictions on it yourself. Don't write more than 30 pages, say, or don't have modules longer than 750 words. You'll find the limits will tighten your focus. If you have a structure that worked for you in the past, keep using it. Create the skeleton, and then you add flesh to the bones.[1]

A good plan is to *chunk down* a big project into manageable pieces. I wrote the first draft of this book over five months. I produced good material from 8 am to 9.30 am and then had a break before a second stint around 10.30 am to noon. I didn't write for longer than that because my energy drops after three hours. I'm quite happy to write over the weekend because I like the sense of momentum, so I usually wrote five or six days a week. I didn't write on days when I was teaching or on holiday but did jot down any ideas that came up.

I estimate that I had 120 mornings to come up with the first draft. I deliberately wrote too much (around 45,000 words) because I like the sense of stripping out and tightening up that comes during the revision phase. My planning told me that I only needed to hit 375 words per day. Chunking down allowed me to track my progress.

So that you get a feel for it, 375 words is the length of this little section. A big smarty-pants like you can write that easily every day.

## Writing will tear you apart, again

Writing wears you out. It's mentally tiring and can lead to a surprising amount of physical pain. Shoulder tension, headaches and eyestrain are all common symptoms of a writer who's pushing it too hard.

Being kind to yourself starts with realistic expectations. No-one can write all day and all night for weeks on end without getting exhausted. No-one writes a perfect first draft. And no-one, despite their boasts on

Instagram, is writing 5,000 fabulous words a day. So be kind to yourself. Aiming for three sentences, a couple of paragraphs or half a module turns the impossible into the achievable. Disconnect from email and social media to create an environment free of distractions. If you're in the office, mark out your territory by putting on headphones or finding a quiet corner. Find the time of day that's best for your writing.

## Early drafts are never perfect

Early drafts of an article or a report are all about getting the words out of your head and onto the page. Your brain is full of facts, opinions, evidence, stories and ideas. You need to clear the mind of all this good stuff before you can revise and shape your work.

When I finished the first draft of *Write Now!* I printed it out and left it in a drawer for a month. That's not some sort of writer's metaphor, but a literal description. At this stage I was far too close to what I'd written to revise it with any sense of perspective. I swung between believing every word was brilliant and every word was crap. Neither of these two mindsets would help me with revising. (This process of print and forget also applied to the second and third drafts.)

You need to experience a similar sense of detachment between the first and revised draft of your work. Writing is about more than just the time when you're sat at your desk or at your favourite table in the cafe. Give your brain the freedom to mull over your thoughts, do more research, get unblocked. When your grandmother told you to sleep on a problem, she knew exactly what she was talking about.

## Where to now?

Chapter 10 – a weird one, but I believe where we write affects our choice of words. I use longer words if I'm in the library, and my style is more informal and chatty when I'm in a café. Does changing location help you find the voice you want?

Chapter 16 – in the chapter you've just read I mentioned some of the apps I use to help me with planning. In chapter 16, I'll talk about some apps I sometimes use to help with writing.

Chapter 17 – when we consider essential polishes I'll talk about how we use different parts of the brain for writing and revising. How can you create different environments for these tasks?

## Note

1 I certainly agonised about this sentence during the revision phase. If you think this is bad, be thankful you'll never see the metaphors I rejected.

# Part 2

# Structure
## The Nuts and Bolts of Writing

# Chapter 5

# Planning and intros

Let me get zen for a moment. *You want your structure to be so clear it becomes invisible to the reader.* Show a clear structure, and readers will trust you to lead them to what's most important.

Take *Write Now!* as an example. It's very structured, but I hope you haven't noticed. Each page of this book contains an average of 21 sentences. I'm asking you to read them, understand them, think about them and then remember them as we move through the chapters. That's a big ask.

Me, the editors and our designer have worked hard to guide you. Each chapter has a header and number. Headlines and subheaders move you through the pages, and different font sizes and the occasional use of italics show you where sections begin and end. Graphs and white space break up big chunks of text. Every chapter ends with the *Where to Now* recommendations, which changes the rhythm of your reading and marks the transition between one chapter and the next.

You *get* good structure by organising your thoughts. You *show* good structure by design. Let's prove this by looking at two contents pages for the same report.

The festival has been extremely successful since its inception and feedback is overwhelmingly positive from all sources. Audience satisfaction remains high, authors are happier than they have ever been, and we see increased buy-in from agents and publicists. Spinoff benefits of the festival include a positive impact on the local economy of £6 million, an increase in social inclusion and stronger partnerships with hotels. A five-year plan is included, as are our contact details.

**Table of Contents**

*Figure 5.1*

DOI: 10.4324/9781003513520-7

Why do we all reject the box on the left? It's a solid, unattractive wall of text. The designers have tried to make it seem less intimidating by switching to friendly italics, but the lack of space makes it impossible to find what we need. Topics are bunched up, sentences are too long and there's no hierarchy to tell us what's important. Printing white on grey looks good for about four words, but then it's exhausting to read. Since the mid-fifteenth century, when Johannes Gutenberg first invented the printing press, we've preferred black on white. You move away from that at your peril.

Why is the Table of Contents on the right better? The structure leaps out at us – there are two meaty sections, with three modules in each. The report is topped and tailed with short sections that seem skimmable. We know our total 'commitment' will be no more than 20 pages and it's also easy for us to find the topics – audience satisfaction, say, or social inclusion – that most interest us.

They sprinkle a handful of design hacks to guide a reader's eyes. You notice the separate headers with bullet points and the bigger font for the title. But that's enough to convince the reader of two very important factors:

1. The writer has control over his material. The ideas have a basis in logic and are presented in a convincing way. Readers trust writers who look organised. Even if they disagree with the arguments, they feel they're in safe hands if they can see organisation.
2. The writer cares about his readers. Content pages are always a pain to write, but they're a pleasure to read because they save so much time. The writer is proving to the reader that he's spent time researching, writing, editing and organising.

Readers will always complain if the structure doesn't work but will rarely complement you if it's good.

### The mind is a structure-seeking missile

Look up at the stars tonight and find the star formation called the Great Bear. It looks nothing like a bear, does it? Ptolemy, an ancient Greek with Roman and Egyptian connections, produced a catalogue of astral constellations that was full of imagined shapes, including Pegasus, Hercules and the frankly disappointing Little Bear. Two millennia later, and we're still using his names.

Why? The human mind instinctively searches for structure. I can give you a list of random words (library, Budapest, crossword) and you'll immediately attempt to categorise them, looking for similarities and connections that don't exist or try to put them all into the same sentence. Don't worry, we all do it.

The reading mind's favourite shape is a pyramid. To understand why, we need to look at the difference between how we form our ideas and how we communicate them. (There's much more on this in Chapter 12.)

### Bottom-up thinking is how you decide

Lucky me! You're taking me out to dinner tonight. It's a surprise treat, so I'm not involved in any of the planning, which leaves you to think about the following variables:

Time – just after work, or shall we meet later?
Place – how close are we? Do we want it walkable or shall we take a taxi? City centre or that little place out in the countryside?
Type of restaurant – by country (Chinese, Italian), by speciality (pork ribs, macrobiotic)
Restrictions – religious rules, diets, allergies, convictions, illnesses
Budget – not an issue tonight since it's your treat.

How do you arrive at your decision? You talk to your friends, ask for recommendations and remember great places you're been in the past. You go to TripAdvisor to compare average ratings, and read reviews in newspapers. If that all works out, you still have to check availability and make a booking. This is the research you have to perform before you can tell me your message.

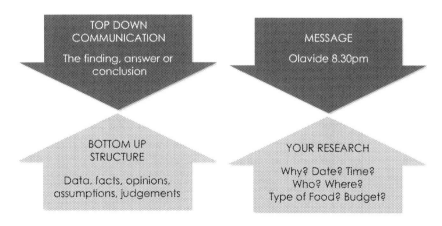

*Figure 5.2*

## The top-down message is what you communicate

You send me your decision – Mama Campo in Plaza Olavide at 8.30pm. I'll see you there.

What's the implication for report writing? Your answer – which you might also call your finding, recommendation, main point or conclusion – comes first. Your report will be a success if the CEO strolling past your desk just reads this and nothing else. Of course, other readers will want to dive deeper into chapters and modules because they want to learn how you arrived at your conclusion. They need to analyse your stats, read your interviews, check your diagrams and perhaps criticise your thought processes.

Your report needs to be flexible enough to work for both the CEO and the deep diver. And that's why the pyramid structure works so well.

## Pyramids reflect how the mind works

They help the reader follow your arguments and also save you tons of time in the planning stage.

Take a look at this pyramid I designed for an analyst's report on the precious metal, Rhodium. The analyst felt swamped by having too much material to include and couldn't find a convincing way to structure her report. We started by making the main message – *Buy Rhodium* – as upfront as possible. It's bold and clear and no-one can miss it up there at the apex. It's the opposite of storytelling, where the ending is only revealed in the final scene. Readers want to know what you found out, not how you found it.

We spoke to the analyst's clients to get guidance on the next level of the pyramid. They helped us immensely by identifying the three areas that interested them – *Price, Supply, Demand*. These three messages below the apex support her main message. The pyramid made it easier for clients to find what they want. Are they mostly concerned by Price? Great, they can jettison the sections on Supply and Demand straightaway.

Below the main sections are modules (which you may also call chapters). Let's say our reader wants to find out more about Demand. He can easily find the analyst's opinions on technology and fashion by moving to the relevant section. And if fashion is his main interest, the information on why rhodium is popular in the luxury jewellery sector is on the next level. It's clear where he can find more about its dazzling shininess and its resistance to corrosion.

It's awful when a reader gets lost. You watch them turn back a page, scratch their head in bewilderment, then tut out loud as they toss your report aside. Signposting stops them getting frustrated. All the way through a report we guide them with headlines, subheaders and formatting.

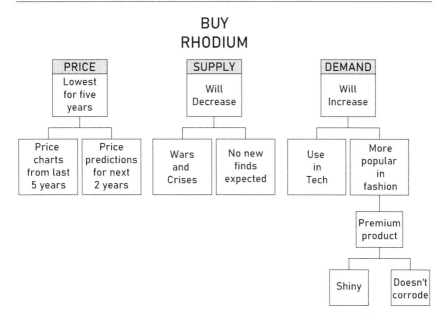

*Figure 5.3*

As she moved lower down the pyramid, the analyst concentrated more on detailed research. This is the place to present evidence, search for flaws in commonly accepted arguments, collect data and crunch numbers. A level below she added statistics on jewellery sales, comparisons to other precious metals like palladium, and pictures of soon-to-be-released Rhodium jewellery.

Don't dismiss the bottom of your pyramid as mere backup information. It proves to readers – especially those who oppose your message – that you can support your argument with evidence and facts. Even your fiercest critic will concede that you've considered the topic in depth, not cobbled together some trash from the internet.

The pyramid structure is essential for your longer pieces of writing. And it'll help you immensely in the planning stage, as you struggle to turn your bottom-up findings into a coherent top-down message.

## The perfectly baked introduction, every time

Many of us hate writing introductions. The blank screen stares accusingly at us, challenging us to turn our thoughts into prose. We scribble something down, press delete and watch mouth agape as our word count hovers around the absolutely zero mark. We're often nervous, because the intro marks the point when our research is over and the writing begins. We can't delay it any longer. It's time to write.

But we can end that unpleasant mix of anxiety and procrastination buzzing in our stomach by taking a tip from charity collectors, who do some of the best introductions you're ever heard. I've been hassled by them in the Zócalo in Mexico City, outside the Gare du Nord in Paris and on the elegant Bahnhofstrasse in the centre of Zurich. With their friendly smiles, bright T-shirts and ever-ready clipboards, the charity collectors are skilled at prising money from the wallets of the world.

Every collector – called a *charity mugger* by their critics, or even a *chugger* by their worst enemies – follows a set plan when they're pitching to commuters hurrying past them. They've got very little time to pique your interest, so they use SCQA to open up the conversation even as you stare doggedly at the pavement and try to spear them with the tip of your umbrella.

| Situation | *It's like this . . .* |
|-----------|------------------------|
| Complication | *. . . .and it's getting worse.* |
| Question | *What can be done?* |
| Answer | *Change feelings, thoughts and actions* |

The SCQA has four elements whose order never changes.

Here's a medical example I heard three days ago:

Situation (S) – more people are waiting for a kidney transplant than ever before.

Complication (C) – many donor families are unable to give the gift of life because they can't find the donor card.

Question (Q) – what can be done to increase the supply of kidneys in an ethical way?

Answer (A) – switch to an opt-out system, where donation is presumed unless stated otherwise.

Every single word works hard to convince the listener. The move from S to C creates a sense of dread and doom. *It's bad, and it's getting worse.* The Q begs an A, creating a conversational flow. The four parts change what you think (*I didn't know so many people were on the waiting list*) and give you a simple way to act *(I can vote in favour of the opt-out system).*

SCQA is a failproof way to start reports. It summarises your most important points and suggests a plan of action. It involves the reader by starting with a situation they recognise, and then increases the conflict with a complication which threatens impending disaster.

You talk directly with the readers when you ask the question – *what can be done?* The reader will be desperate for your answer. The A in the SCQA should be on the front cover of all your reports from now on.

## Where to now?

Chapters 5–8 – I've put a secret structure in these Nuts and Bolts chapters. I'm moving from big to small. So we started with overall structure, followed by paragraphs and sentences, then grammar and punctuation and, finally, words.

Chapter 6 – structure goes all the way down to the sentence level. We'll look at ways to make your sentences instantly stronger.

## Exercise

Find examples of SCQA in pitch documents, newspaper articles, blog posts and the blurbs on the back of books. Which ones work, which ones don't? Challenge yourself to take one of the poor ones and make it better.

# Chapter 6

# Paragraphs and sentences

It's frustrating to read short, random lines of text that have no logic or coherence. And it's exhausting to read page after page of text in solid blocks. Be realistic. Perfect paragraphs probably don't exist, but your readers will thank you for trying.

Paragraph construction is often neglected by business writers. They spend so much time on the *macro* (content, structure) and the *micro* (headings, word choice) that they believe the paragraphs will take care of themselves. That rarely happens. Luckily, there are quick and easy techniques that make your paragraphs more appealing.

## How to design a paragraph

A typical paragraph has three elements.

### 1. Topic sentence

This is the key idea you want to get across. A good topic sentence exists without the rest of the paragraph. Imagine someone scanning your article as they're waiting for the bus. If they read *paragraph construction is often neglected by business writers* they get a full idea of what you want to tell them. I'm not saying the rest of the paragraph is irrelevant, just that the topic sentence is the one they should remember. It sets up what comes next.

You might want to start the topic sentence with a linking word (see later) but don't feel obliged.

### 2. Supporting sentence(s)

These back up your topic sentence. Here's where you put the examples that illustrate your opinion, the statistics and the data that confirm it. It's the place for the evidence and quotes that convince the reader to see the world from your point of view.

DOI: 10.4324/9781003513520-8

Where do you put the ideas that contradict your supporting sentences? I recommend you put them in a separate paragraph, which begins with a link along the lines of *some people disagree with this approach* or *on the other hand.*

### 3. Closing sentence

You've got to show logic here. The closing sentence either wraps up the current paragraph or leads into the next.

If the closing sentence doesn't feel like it belongs, then no amount of verbal tinkering will lead to a smooth transition. A clumsy or awkward sentence is usually the sign that you should change how you link your arguments.

Without getting too meta, I'll close this sentence about closing paragraphs by linking to the next section, which is about linking paragraphs.

## How to link paragraphs

These transition words and phrases guide the reader. It's a little bit like listening to fairy tales. We trust people who know how to use *once upon a time, and then, finally* and *they all lived happily after.* We feel we're in safe hands because they know exactly the right moment for the wolf to reveal his teeth.

I've split these transition words into three groups.

### 1. Simple Links

It's often enough to use a conjunction like *but, however* and *although* to move the reader through a paragraph. Don't be afraid of using ordinals (*first up, secondly, the third case of this*) in supporting sentences or as a way of starting the next paragraph. The classics of storytelling – *firstly, then, next, finally* – are great to lead a reader through a complicated process or a lengthy timeline.

### 2. Adding additional information

You don't need anything more complicated than *also* or *similarly* when you're sharing evidence which supports your ideas. The slightly formal *moreover* and *furthermore* can also be used. *In addition* is a smooth way to introduce more examples.

Sometimes, when I'm really stuck for inspiration, I'll pull out the phrase *this is a good place to talk about.* It's surprising just how effective it can be.

### 3. Introducing a different point of view

This is a good place to talk about how to introduce dissenting arguments. Phrases you could use include *looking at the problem from their point of view* and the more informal *if I was in their shoes*. But you can also be sneaky and introduce their perspective in a phrase which suggests you don't value it. There's something intrinsically dismissive about introducing a sentence with *our critics believe* or *to play devil's advocate*.

## Ideal paragraph length doesn't exist

Context is everything. There's a difference between sending a text to your buddies and writing your doctorate. Well, there should be.

I'm a three- or four-sentence guy when it comes to my paragraphs. I'll use a one-sentence paragraph to change the rhythm and surprise your eyes. And very occasionally, I'll write six or seven sentences to give the piece a more discursive air, as if I were dressed in velvet smoking jacket and leaning on a marble fireplace, telling you stories about my life as a double agent.

If you write too many short paragraphs, you run the risk of people assuming you don't know your subject in depth. This is the feeling you get when you scan through a clickbait article on *7 Things Every Writer Needs to Keep on Their Desk*. But if your paragraphs are too long you might come across as a person who doesn't know how to share their knowledge and who doesn't care that readers have to struggle through the dense thickets of their prose.

## The best sentences reflect how the brain works

We like short, self-contained units that express a single idea, rather than four-line monsters filled with contradictions and caveats. The most effective sentence length is a paltry eight words, and short words are always preferred over long. It's always easy to see where a writer has got tired or bored because the sentences become flabby.

But here are five-sentence structures that keep your writing crisp and sharp, especially when you're feeling the exact opposite. They send out a strong message that your sentence construction – and, consequently, your thinking – is logical. They're effective because they mirror how the majority of readers think.

### 1. We see the past to our left

Here's a game to play with a friend. Ask them to remember the colour of their school gate or the pealing of the school bell. About 90% of people will move their eyes to the left as they access their memory. Sometimes their head will turn to the left as well.

Let's use this to our advantage when constructing sentences. If we're explaining how something used to be done, it's always best to start with the past and move into the now.

☑ Last year our best sales were in the north, but this year turnover is much higher in the south

If you reverse the pattern (going from now to the past), it seems clunky and less natural.

☒ This year turnover is much higher in the south, but last year our best sales were in the north

### 2. We see the future to our right

Ask the same friend to tell you about their dream holiday. Watch amazed as they move their eyes to the right, where most of us see the future. About 90% of people turn to their right side as they imagine the view over the harbour and the waves on the beach.

Once more, the brain tells us how to write. If we're explaining what's going to happen, it's a more logical and pleasant read to start with the now and move into the future.

☑ Net income has held steady this year in the east but is forecast to grow next year in the west

Turning this natural pattern around produces a sentence that doesn't flow as well.

☒ Net income is forecast to grow next year in the west but has held steady this year in the east

### 3. When we read about a problem, we expect to be told the solution

Readers become uncomfortable if you make them wait for the answer to an issue you've raised. Problem/solution sentences are popular because they have a natural logic. They reflect a reader's natural desire to see a conclusion.

☑ We don't have enough staff to maximise our opportunities, so it's a good move to increase headcount in marketing

If you reverse the order, you're giving the answer before the problem and that doesn't flow as smoothly.

☒ It's a good move to increase headcount in marketing, because we don't have enough staff to maximise our opportunities.

### 4. If/then

This pattern is the best way to write about cause and effect. It's most common form is *if x, then y*.

☑ If we move the main office to Kerala, the staff members left behind in Birmingham will be miserable

Reversing the natural order to give *then y, if x* isn't wrong but it reads clumsy.

☒ The staff members left behind in Birmingham will be miserable, if we move the main office to Kerala

### 5. Compare and contrast

This is especially for those of you in the financial world, or anyone who has to understand budgets and cashflows. If you give people a number or a percentage on its own, they're likely to feel a bit lost.

☒ Operating costs are $82 million
☒ Our net profit margin is 9.2%

It's more meaningful if we provide comparisons, either in the form of absolute numbers or as ratios and percentages.

☑ Operating costs are $82 million (down from $94 million last year)
☑ Our net profit margin is 9.2% (8.3% last year).

Incidentally, this is a place where you can ignore my advice on eye movements in 1 and 2 above. It's normal to have the comparison in brackets directly after this year's number. Just make sure it's clear to the reader whether the comparative is from last year or is the estimate for the next year.

These compare and contrast sentences are not unique to finance. You'll see them when people are comparing sizes, populations, grades, wellbeing measures, economic indicators, distances and lots of other factors.

## Where to now?

Chapter 3 – remind yourself how readers choose which writers to follow.

Chapter 14 – clarity is the one factor that all readers demand. Find out why in this chapter.

Chapter 18 – summary writing skills will help you write even better. This is an area that's often skimped in business writing books, but it's essential.

Chapter 7

# Grammar and punctuation

## My plea for grammar

Language is organic and forever changing. I'm suspicious of the pedants who look up grammar rules in dusty Victorian tomes to win an argument. I don't value people who stick to rules that are better broken.

But I don't think grammar rules should be ignored. Stick with them, and in most cases, your message will be clearer and have more impact. And clarity and impact are two of the objectives we agreed on way back in the first chapter.

Over the millennia of their existence, languages have worked hard for us. Grammar is an essential component of language, evolving as we speed up our communications. Our language rules are not always perfect – I've never understood how we ended up with three spellings for *two, too* and *to* when the words sound exactly the same. But imagine the alternative, where everything was a free for all.

Looking for a quick example of how bad grammar weakens your message? Look no closer than this advert for an online training company.

## Quality Courses

All our courses are build and proofread by industry
professionals who are experts in there chosen field

DOI: 10.4324/9781003513520-9

Even if you don't notice bad grammar, spelling, editing, proofreading and all that writerly stuff, you'll feel at a subconscious level that something is wrong with this sentence. And if you do know when to use *their, there* or *they're*, you won't go any further into the website. We make decisions online very quickly, so why give people an easy way to reject you?

This is a genuine ad, so I won't mention the company's name (or point out they used the wrong tense of *build* as well).

## Whom you going to call? Grammar busters!

Correct grammar sends out three signals to readers:

1. The writer cares about the reader – we associate bad grammar with a lack of respect and professionalism.
2. The writer has control over her content – sloppiness tells us that the writer doesn't know the topic and/or can't express themself.
3. The writer has revised and edited – obvious errors tell us the piece has been rushed and is likely to be low quality.

But first, I have to get something off my chest. Lots of people who correct your grammar don't have any idea what they're talking about. And sometimes their motivations are suspect. Are they stuck in the past, driven by ancient rules that never existed? Perhaps they are being finickety (or is that pernickety?) just to annoy you.

Let's look at the five types of people you meet in grammar hell

1. People who confuse their personal preferences for rules. These are the people who insist you use *whilst* not *while* and tell you off for writing *The Guardian* instead of 'the Guardian'. Don't listen to them, unless they present you with a company style guide or they pay your invoices.
2. The-stuck-in-the-muds. They think grammar rules were carved in stone and then displayed next to the Magna Carta. They're wrong. If you're in a masochistic frame of mind, buy a selection of grammar books and see how they differ on everyday expressions like *Me and Dave* and *Dave and I*. (Better still, save your money and trust that I have researched this.)
3. The weird online snobs. You occasionally see someone attacking the arguments of another person by complaining about their grammar. *Why should I listen to your points when you can't even use commas properly, eh?* Pointing out the punctuation and grammar errors of other people is rarely the way to make friends. And once you've put yourself forward as a grammar guru, your new enemy will watch you like a hawk, ready to swoop on your mistakes.

4. The fearsome feedbackers. If you're editing someone else's work, be mindful of how sensitive people can be. No-one likes being pulled-up for their mistakes, so show some kindness when someone asks you to check their work. And take the time to explain why changes need to be made, rather than just drowning their writing in red ink.

5. People who insist on ordering *two whoppers juniors* in Burger King. Just don't.

> Grammar – like language – changes all the time. Business language isn't controlled by rule enforcers like the Académie Française. It reacts instantly to new words and ideas. It's the same with grammar. Hast thou got that?

## The greatest hits of punctuation and grammar

Grammar is a big topic, so I'm going to focus on the areas where people most commonly screw up. I want you to think less about rules and more about the quest for clarity.

## A quick whizz through punctuation

I reckon I can teach you all you need to know about punctuation in the next five pages. And I'll shoehorn in the worst joke you've heard in your life. Let the challenge begin!

A personal note. I'm halfway through Peter Jackson's eight-hour documentary on the Beatles. *Get Back* is great, and it's occupying a lot of my brain space. It's going to have an impact on some of my examples.

## Apostrophes that show possession

You learned this in school when you were nine, so I forgive you if you've forgotten. It's simple.

Allen Klein manages the Beatles. He is *the band's manager.*

Allen Klein manages the Beatles and the Stones. He is *the bands' manager.*

## Apostrophes for names ending in s

There's only one tricky area with apostrophes, and that's with names ending in s. I'm happy for you to refer to this as *Andreas's brilliant book* or *Andreas' brilliant book*. Trust me, I don't mind.

If you're called Agnes, and you and your two best mates (who are also called Agnes) are considering opening a restaurant together, be careful. The use of apostrophes when two or more people have the same name is a subject best avoided. Just call it *The Seaside Café* and no grammarians will get hurt.

## Colons (:)

Use them to introduce a list. *John Lennon plays three instruments: guitar, bass and piano.*

And occasionally you can use them when you want to highlight how a second clause[1] links to a first. The colon directs the reader to new information which supports the first half of the sentence. *The band had two choices when the police realised Harrison was underage: they could fight the case or head back to England.*

Other than that, avoid them. They look awkward on a screen, they're hard to get right, and they'll mark you out as slightly old fashioned.

## Commas

We use commas in three main ways:[2]

1. It's where we would pause if we were speaking. *Their relationship, problematic at the best of times, was tested by Clapton's infatuation with George's wife.*
2. It's how we separate items in a list. *The Beatles' inner circle included Yoko, Linda, Mal Evans and roadie Ken Harrington.*
3. It's how we add extra information, a bit like using brackets. *The rehearsals, run by Ken Harrington, began slowly.*

## Emojis and exclamation marks

Every grammar book will tell you not to use them. But texting and tweeting have altered how we communicate, and only a fool would fail to notice that people use smiley faces all the time. This might come as a surprise but I encourage you to add some of these to your writing. But only if you consider two factors: context and client.

### Context

Making loads of people redundant, or sending out directions for a funeral? Best give the emojis a rest.

Language always has a context. There's a difference between posting a gig review on Twitter – *a banging nite out!* 🎉 👜 – and submitting your resume for the management trainee scheme at the World Bank. You wouldn't turn up for a formal interview in your trainers, so why add a row of purple kisses to your acceptance letter?

Client

One of the agencies I work with is staffed by people in their twenties and thirties. I was baffled by their initial communications – why did *how are you?* need to be *how are you???!!* Since when had *I agree* been replaced with 👍 and *good work* with 👏? But then I thought, why not? Instead of getting all huffy and puffy, I accepted that this is nothing more than a modern way to communicate. I started to use emojis in my replies and since then I've felt more comfortable speaking with them. And that, in turn, has led to more fees!!!! $😊$ ♡$ ✨

## It's vs. its

I see loads of people screwing this up, which is a shame, because all you need to do is remember these two points.

1. *It's* is the short way of writing *it is*. Nothing else. We use it all the time – *it's raining today, it's seventy kilos of drinking pleasure, it's about time we left.*
2. *Its* indicates possession. *I bought the book because of its great cover.* Some people (not you, obvs) expect an apostrophe because we write *the book's great cover.* But we can't use the apostrophe, because of point 1 above.

## The -ing form

Here's an easy win for you in the quest to be concise. Lots of business writers choose *I will be talking about this* over *I'll talk about this.* They think it makes them appear more professional, but often it just adds unneeded syllables that get in the way of your message. Keep it simple, and ditch the – ing form.

## Pride capitals

These are the extra capitals that signify that you think someone's role is really important and/or you love them. *He was then the Director of EMI and CEO.* They're not needed, even on your resume. Especially not on your resume.

## Scare quotes

These are the quotation marks you put around a word to draw attention to it. They're now universally understood to be a shorthand for *so-called,* and they send out the message that the writer is being ironic or disbelieving. *Ringo's entire 'contribution' to the album was a thirty-second piano riff that George turned into a full song.* You can almost imagine the speaker raising an eyebrow and flicking air quotes around the word *contribution*.

Avoid scare quotes if you're not being sarcastic or nasty. Far better to underline or italicise the word that's important to you.

## Semicolons (;)

Some people use these to link two clauses. Both clauses have to be complete sentences, and there has to be a reason to link them. *George Harrison wasn't treated well by Lennon and McCartney; they'd always seen him as an inferior songwriter.*

If you do feel tempted to use a semicolon, the second clause doesn't take a capital letter (unless it's a proper name like *Liverpool or Apple*).

Let's face facts. Colons and semicolons are going the same way as the ampersand (&). If a sentence is too long, we either split it with a comma or divide it into two.

Most people under the age of 35 automatically associate colons and semicolons with a smiley face, rather than a punctuation mark (:)). That's just one more reason to avoid them.

## So at the beginning of a sentence

Strictly speaking, this is neither grammar nor punctuation but I want to scream at you not to do it and this is the only place in the book I can do it.

It's usually unneeded. *So, I enjoyed watching the documentary.* And it gives the impression that you are hesitant and unsure of what you are about to write. But if it's generally a linking word, keep it as a shorter alternative to *therefore*.

## When to use *that* and when to use *which*

When you're speaking this is simple because no-one cares! The distinction between *that* and *which* is so fine that no-one complains when we mix them up.

When you're writing, however, it's good to show you know the difference.

*That* introduces new information that's essential. *George Martin edited the tapes that became the album* tells us more than *George Martin edited the tapes.*

*Which* introduces new information that isn't vital to the reader's understanding. *The single, which was Linda's favourite track, reached number 1 in 24 countries.* The detail between the commas is a nice to know but isn't essential.

A tip for you. Read your sentence aloud. If you pause before giving new information, you probably need *which*. If you continue without taking a breath, choose *that*.

## Your vs. you're

*Your* shows possession of something. *Your solo album is great, your drugs are psychedelic.*

You're is a short way to write *you are*. For example, *you're going on tour, you're taking too many of those drugs.*

Here's that joke I threatened earlier. I know you've been waiting for it all chapter, and I can only apologise in advance.

Q What's the difference between *your dinner* and *you're dinner?*

A One leaves you nourished. The other leaves you dead.

Get it? Appalling, I know. But it's stuck in your memory now, and that means you'll always get it right from now on.

## Where to now?

Chapter 10 – grammar is also a component of your writing style and voice. Different brands have different approaches to colons and clauses. What works for the Metropolitan Museum of Art in New York might not work for the Port Authority.

Chapter 14 – if you're huffing and puffing about a grammar rule, consider why we have grammar. Your number one priority is clarity, not keeping the online trolls happy.

## Have you thought about this?

George Harrison wrote a song called *I Me Mine*. Many music critics believe it's about the spiritual dangers inherent in materialism, but us grammar types know different.

## Notes

1  A clause is a group of words that forms a complete sentence. *Ringo plays the drums* is a clause, *Ringo's drums* isn't.
2  Ha! An example of the correct use of the colon. But it looks odd next to the footnote number, doesn't it?

# Chapter 8

# Words and meaning

You can tell a bad writer by their choice of words. Poor writers believe big businessey words make them sound more authoritative. They don't. No-one is going to trust you more just because you've written *purchase* instead of *buy* or used *robust* and *maximal* a lot in your emails.

Our word choices are shaped by the colleagues around us, the jobs we've had in the past, the subjects we studied at school and the place we've lived. (That's pretty much everything in our life, isn't it?) The good news is that it's easy to improve your writing vocabulary. This chapter is full of very easy wins.

## Watch out for bizspeak

You can't copy the clichés of bizspeak without coming across as unoriginal and unconvincing. Too many meaningless words mean that you'll be tuned out. We laugh at people who pepper their writing with *actionable bandwidth, mission-critical* and *paradigm shift*, but most of us are secretly afraid of falling into these traps.

I've just put the kettle on. In the time it takes to make a coffee, I'll find seven examples of bizspeak on LinkedIn *and* came up with more human alternatives. It takes very little effort to cut out *synergise* and *right-size* but you have to recognise just how perniciously these phrases creep into our everyday language.

You'll see this bizspeak rubbish cluttering up communication all around the world. Try this from WeWork's IPO prospectus:

We are a community company committed to maximum global impact. Our mission is to elevate the world's consciousness.

*Elevate the world's consciousness?* Silly me, I thought you rented out offices.

The irony is that people who are higher up the corporate ladder[1] rarely

DOI: 10.4324/9781003513520-10

resort to bizspeak. People who feel secure in their position prioritise the clarity of their writing over jargon. Using too much bizspeak actually lowers your status. It can also make you sound very dated. If you're reading this ten years after I've written it, are people still using *agile, thought leader* and *the new normal?* I suspect not.

*Table 8.1 Use human language instead of bizspeak*

| LinkedIn says | But you should write |
| --- | --- |
| Going forward | In the future |
| | Next |
| Brings to the table | Gives |
| | Provides |
| Pull the trigger | Commit (I think this is what it means) |
| | Start |
| Reach out | Contact |
| | Call |
| | Write |
| It is what it is | I think this means *get over it* or *let's move on*, but I'm not sure |
| Touch base | Talk to |

Jargon is like a suit, a car, or a watch – it's a status symbol. Those who are insecure 'dress up' their words, believing it will make them appear smarter or cause others to take them more seriously.
– Adam Galinsky, professor at Columbia Business School, who researched how pompous word choice often reflects a writer's lack of confidence.

## Beginner's Latin doesn't make you a better writer

One of my favourite words is *quintessence*. I love how it turns my lips into a kiss, then a smile, then a kiss again. It sounds great as well, the thrust of the *qu* followed by the soft, sibilant *sss*. But most of all I love it because it makes me sound really smart – or so I used to think.

There's a long tradition of people deliberately choosing words of Latin origin to make them sound more intelligent. Think doctors, stuffy officials and, of course, pompous politicians. But over the years it's dawned on me that multisyllabic words create problems in writing. They may make you seem arrogant and patronising, and they also take up a lot of space on the page. Some readers won't know what they mean, which is a sure-fire way to annoy them.

It is far better to choose a shorter, punchier alternative. English always has a one or two syllable replacement that readers prefer. I dropped *quintessence* and replaced it with *gist*.[2]

Here's a list of some changes that immediately improve your readability.

Table 8.2 Prefer Anglo-Saxon words over their Latin equivalents

| Your Latin teacher said | But you should write |
| --- | --- |
| Assistance | Help |
| Commencement | Begin, start |
| Discontinue | End, stop |
| Magnitude | Size |
| Necessitate | Need |
| Purchase | Buy |
| Regulation | Rule |

## Legal language belongs in the courts

The lawyers I know are great at writing agreements and brilliant at public speaking. They've been schooled to use language in a very precise way. The words and phrases they bandy about in dusty court rooms are very specific to them, even if they appear arcane and impenetrable to us.

Some writers believe that sprinkling a few legal-sounding phrases across their writing will help their argument. Don't copy them. Phrases like *ex post facto* and *sine qua non* have no place in your writing, unless you actually are a lawyer. People use them because they mistakenly believe this vocabulary makes them appear intelligent. But adding *as previously advised* and *without prejudice* to your emails makes you sound odd and awkward, like a man proclaiming *herewith a round of drinks* to his mates in the pub.

The indiscriminate use of legal-sounding words makes you seem old fashioned and out of step. The last person who needed to add *thus* to a sentence was Queen Victoria. Avoid.

## The language of local government and the third sector

The charity I founded, The Margate Bookie, spreads a love of reading and writing around a town that's a bizarre mix of rich incomers, poor locals, trendy artists and happy-go-lucky chancers. I'm happy to say that I never had any contact with the local council, other than the occasional tut as

*Table 8.3 Leave legalese in the courts*

| Your lawyer says | But you should write |
| --- | --- |
| At this present moment | Now |
| Regarding | About |
| In advance of | Before |
| In the event that | If |
| In order to | To (It's exactly the same) |
| In relation with | About |
| For the purpose of | To |

I tried to understand the baffling dustbin schedule. All this changed when I started to apply for funding for the charity.

I didn't understand any of the emails I got. The syntax was convoluted and confusing, and I had to decipher them line by line. And the choice of words? The worst I've ever come across. I felt the council was putting up a linguistic barrier between me and them. I was lost, and I wasn't sure that was accidental. I had terrifying flashbacks to a French exam that I hadn't prepared for. I needed a translator.

I investigated further and came across the Local Government Association, who have listed over two hundred words and phrases that hinder communication between local councils and the people they are meant to serve. There's no space to reproduce the whole list, but among the humdingers you'll find *best practice, citizen empowerment, core values, improvement levers* and *joined up thinking*. It's sad to see that so many of these were outdated bizspeak terms 20 years ago. So be wary. If you find yourself writing about the *upward trend in strategic priorities for sustainable communities*, it's a fair bet that your reader will hate you. Unless they're in a *trialogue* with some *place-shapers*.

## The extra words we never need

First drafts are usually peppered with words that are unnecessary. I've identified five areas for us to think about.

### The qualifying adjectives that add nothing

These include *absolutely, actually, a little bit, very, really* and *quite*. I find a lot of these in my first drafts. (I think it's because I use a lot of them when I'm talking.) I only leave them in if they're absolutely[3] necessary.

You can use them, of course, but make sure you really, really need them. Which you normally don't.

Table 8.4 Delete unneeded qualifiers

| Qualifier | Replace with |
| --- | --- |
| Very | Blank space |
| Rather | Nothing |
| A bit | Do you see . . . |
| Quite | . . . where we are going with this? |

### The spare that

You'll see this a lot in unpolished business writing. There's no semantic difference between these two sentences.

☑ the organisation you represent
☒ the organisation that you represent

No-one will notice if you cut 'that' from the second example.

### Personal tags

Be careful of tags like *IMHO* or *for me*. People are reading you for your opinion, and it's obvious that your writing represents your point of view. (*You* in this sense refers to either you as an individual or the organisation you represent.) Adding phrases such as *it's my belief that* is like saying *I am shaking your hand* while shaking someone's hand. It's unnecessary and odd.

### Helping verbs

These extra verbs often get in the way of clear meaning – I *hope* to prove, this report *aims* to show, we will *try* to explain. Cut them out to save word count. As a by-product, you will sound more confident and in control.

### Redundant words in phrases we use all the time

Looking to trim the flesh from your writing? Get rid of unnecessary words in common phrases.

*Table 8.5 Watch out for redundant words*

| | |
|---|---|
| Advance notice, warning, planning | Of course they're in advance. What point is there warning people about a volcanic eruption after it's happened? |
| Sudden surprise, unexpected surprise | Because what surprise isn't sudden or unexpected? |
| Past history | All history is in the past . . . |
| New innovations | . . . and all innovations are new |
| Plan ahead, plan for the future | Because only a right idiot plans for the past |
| Difficult dilemma | If your decision is easy, you don't face a dilemma but a choice |
| Postpone until later | Unless this is a meeting about a time travel machine |

## Where to now?

Chapter 4 – go back to our ideas on mindset. See them as a way of moving away from the default of bizspeak.

Chapter 17 – editing and proofing is where you'll catch many of these verbal clangers. It takes time and effort to chop the bizspeak, but it will be worth it.

An exercise for you. Take a look at this extract from Steve Easterbrook, the former CEO of McDonalds. Underline every business cliché.

*The immediate priority for our business is restoring growth under a new organizational structure and ownership mix designed to provide greater focus on the customer, improve our operating fundamentals and drive a recommitment to running great restaurants. As we turn around our business, we will look to create more excitement around the brand and ensure that we build on our rich heritage of positively impacting the communities we serve. The first critical step of our operational growth-led plan is to strengthen our effectiveness and efficiency to drive faster and more customer-led decisions. We will restructure our business into four new segments that combine markets with similar needs, challenges, and opportunities for growth.*

*It's drivel, isn't it?*

It's as if Easterbrook didn't actually have a strategy for the business, so he threw a load of business phrases at a piece of paper and hoped they'd find an order. This type of writing communicates a lack of understanding and mental clarity. Cut it out!

## Notes

1 God, it's so easy to slip into bizspeak.
2 Those of you paying attention will have noticed me slipping *gist* into Chapter 7.
3 Itself a target for the red editing pen.

# Part 3

# Influence

## You Can Always Get What You Want

# Chapter 9

# Persuasion, connection, influence

Readers need to make choices every day. We're bombarded with adverts, instructions, suggestions and messages. Most of the time we use mental shortcuts – *I've enjoyed this newspaper a thousand times before, so I believe I will enjoy it today*. We're also a bit lazy. As a consequence, we tend to rely on the status quo, and that makes it hard for writers to break through with a new message.

You can attempt to change what people think, feel and do through laws (the fine for chewing gum in Singapore starts at $500 for a first offence) or education (the *slip-slop-slap* campaign reduced skin cancers among young people in Australia by 5% every year in the nineties and noughties). But most people are moved by *nudges*. These are instructions, sometimes open but usually covert, that guide us towards a desired outcome. It's almost as if the nudge, the way a message is presented, is making the decision for us . . .

But first, lunch with a friend. Beatrice's profile on LinkedIn describes her as a *menu engineer and fundraising specialist*. I'm intrigued as she points out the nudges on the lunch menu at a highly rated fish restaurant overlooking the sunny harbour.

*The decoy item*. Caviar and blinis are an eye-popping £195. A waiter tells us they sell only one of these a month. But the decoy dish convinces people that this is an expensive place, so when we see that scrambled eggs and salmon are £15 we think it's a bargain.

*Currency signs*. The caviar is actually listed at 195, and the scrambled eggs are 15. There's a reason why the trend to drop currency signs is spreading. People will spend up to 30% more when their mind associates a meal with an emotional experience, rather than a financial transaction.

*Daily special*. The restaurant only sells turbot on Tuesdays. This makes it seem scarce, and scarcity always drives sales because people don't want to miss out. Cleverly, the turbot is simultaneously a high-volume item (lots of people order it on Tuesday) that's sold at a premium price (because it's special). Ker-ching!

DOI: 10.4324/9781003513520-12

*Negative space.* Our eyes are drawn to the white space and black border around the haddock, chips and mushy peas. Clever design gives visual prominence to the highest margin meal on the menu.

*Order of items.* The restaurant lists seven starters. People normally choose the first two items or the last item from any list. The restaurant puts its most profitable options (cockles, smoked eel) at the top of the list but ends with its most expensive (king prawns). They know that anything in the middle tends to be glanced over.

Beatrice and I share oysters and order a bottle of wine. She tells me about the nudges that fundraisers use to make donations larger and more frequent. We live in a world that's *decision-noisy*, where people suffer from *compassion fatigue* and *donor burnout*, where *behavioural linguists* advise charities on their *strategic messaging impact*. I'm a bit fuzzy at this stage, but here's what Beatrice tells me while we wait for our main course.

'Timing your message is super-important. No-one likes being asked for money when they're rushing to work, but ask on a summer's day or a holiday and purses will open. Reminding people is also vital. You need to send prompts every so often to encourage donors to repeat their giving. People like to be consistent, so the most generous people are usually those who have given before.'

'Don't abandon your donor just because you've got their money. That's rude, as well as dumb. Send them personalised messages of thanks and show them how their gift has been used. Five lines explaining how their money has changed someone's life has far more impact than a dull report. Make your message quotable, something your donors will be proud to forward to their contacts. The principle of social influence will mean their peers will conform to societal norms . . . .'

'Eh?'

'Get them to tell their mates so they donate as well.'

'Ah. With you.'

That's all very interesting, you're (hopefully) saying to yourself. But how does all this affect your writing? Here are four nudges to add to your writing now.

## 1. Simplicity

Make your paragraphs more readable, the sentences shorter, the words more informal. This isn't dumbing down, but you are consciously putting time and effort into creating a message that is easily understood. Using contractions always helps. The switch from *I cannot help you* to *I can't help you* saves your reader time and also makes you come across as friendly.

## 2. Pronoun power

If you want a client to feel part of a movement, use *we* and *us*. If you want them to feel they're in a dialogue, use *you* and *your*. You can get a text that says *the vaccine will be available tomorrow* or *your vaccine is waiting for you*. It's the second message that makes you roll up your sleeve.

## 3. Exact numbers

It's more persuasive to write *this chapter will make your writing 9.92% better* rather than *this chapter will make your writing 10% better*. The weirdly exact number gets more buy-in because readers think it's more authentic. Rounding numbers up or down makes them less memorable and somehow less convincing. If I tell you that Mount Everest is 8,848.48 metres high, your mind creates a picture of me wearing mountaineering gear and holding some complicated measuring equipment in my icy hands. But if I say it's 8,850 metres, you know I've just looked it up.

## 4. Write in the Now

Use the present tense to make a stronger impact. Promises to lose weight over the next 90 days, or to save for retirement in 30 years, automatically make us think of the future, rather than the present. We therefore find it easier to put off the decision. Better to make people think of immediate gratification – *gain muscle now, start investing today* – than give them an excuse to procrastinate.

Ever been to a hypnotherapist? They frame their instructions in the present (*you are relaxed about flying*) rather than hinting at a vague time in the future (*you will be relaxed about flying*).

'When does nudge become manipulation?'

A cynical and slightly tipsy Beatrice provides a possible answer. 'It's only manipulation if your target notices'. She laughs, but suddenly turns serious. 'It's very hard to get back a reader's trust if they realise they've being deceived by your words'.

You can irritate your readers if you nudge too much or too obviously. Here are three instances of where I've been annoyed by an attempt to nudge me into acting or thinking in a way I didn't like.

### 1. The command that isn't

This is a method that 'softens' an instruction, so it meets less resistance from the reader. *Would you like to clear that mess up?* and *can you come to the meeting in formal wear?* seem like questions but are actually commands.

## 2. The question that isn't

I remember, way back in my radical student days, being immensely irritated by a leaflet from British Nuclear Fuels Limited which asked *why is nuclear power necessary?* The answers that readers came up with weren't important. What the company was actually trying to make us accept was the idea that *nuclear power is necessary.*

## 3. The choice that isn't

This occurs when a command is hidden by the illusion of choice. *Would you like to pay cash or with a credit card?* is a way of closing a sale dressed up as polite customer service.

It's time for pudding. The final course usually provides restaurants with high-margin sales. We listen to the different approaches used by the waiters as they attempt to nudge customers into buying more.

*Would you like pudding?*

A customer can answer no to this question and it won't feel awkward.

*What would you like for pudding?*

This presupposes that a customer is having pudding, so replying with *nothing* makes them seem a little mean-spirited.

*I recommend the meringue nests. Would you like them with strawberries or ice cream? Or both?*

The customer is guided towards today's special. The waiter's question seems to be about choice but is actually designed to sell the meringues (which are delicious, by the way). It also provides an opportunity for the waiter to up-sell extra ice cream.

## The four most valuable words in the world

Sometimes a nudge is so successful, and lasts for such a long time, that the whole world forgets it's being influenced.

## What do you think about when you think about diamonds?

They are an ancient symbol of eternal love. They are expensive to produce, so they must be a high-value investment. They represent glamour, wealth and long-term commitment. They're a girl's best friend. Without them, an engagement seems incomplete and somehow hollow.

Right?

Wrong.

Diamonds are stones. They're good for industrial drilling and, with a heap of polishing and cutting and the right light, they sparkle. It's strange that buying them is proof of the depth of a lover's passion, rather than their gullibility. The world has been conned into paying a fortune for a shiny illusion.

Before 1870, diamonds were rare treasures. They had only been found in Indian riverbeds and deep in the jungles of Latin America. But a huge find in South Africa yielded tons of the things. Investors and miners knew that a sudden glut of diamonds would destroy prices. So, they joined forces to create what would eventually become De Beers Consolidated Mines, one of the most powerful – and most lucrative – monopolies the earth has ever seen.

De Beers has always been a skilful teller of tales. When the market for diamonds collapsed during the Great Depression, De Beers launched a campaign that explicitly connected the price of an engagement ring with the buyer's salary. The ads suggested that one month's salary was an ideal spend. At this time over 90% of rings were bought by men, though nearly all the ads were, of course, placed in women's magazines.

De Beers controlled the world's supply of diamonds. Their strategy was to change how we thought and felt about their not-particularly-precious gems. Their ad agency, N.W. Ayer, designed a series of adverts featuring diamonds next to works of art by Picasso and Dali. These adverts ran in high-class magazines (*Fortune, Vogue, The New Yorker*) where the power of association turned diamonds into a symbol of sophistication. Buying them was akin to buying a famous work of art.

A new narrative had been created by De Beers' PR department. They planted stories in the press about couples separated by war or bad luck whose love was commemorated in their rings. Readers believed that diamonds had been an essential element of an engagement since time immemorial, even though the tradition had been dreamt up in a Manhattan boardroom.

### A diamond is forever

It's copywriter Frances Gerety who's responsible for our perception of diamonds. Her four words, inscribed next to a picture of a couple on honeymoon, has become the most famous advertising slogan of all time. Diamonds are now symbolic of ever-lasting love and Gerety's four words have created billions and billions of dollars in sales. Sure, the slogan has created guilt, envy and immeasurable emotional stress over the last 70 years, but think about the shareholder returns!

And there's a second meaning to *forever*. No-one should ever sell their diamond. Not only would it be a betrayal of love, but it would destroy the illusion that these gemstones possess huge intrinsic value. A brutal ten minutes of negotiation in any downtown second-hand jewellery shop will teach you just how much mark-up is made when love has gone.

> *The diamond engagement ring is de rigueur virtually worldwide,*
> *and the diamond by far the precious gemstone of choice*
>
> - Advertising Age-Slogan of the Century Award, 1999

## Where to now?

Chapter 15 – we all love people who tell good stories. We look at how one brand, Fever-Tree, actually created its own mythology.

Chapter 19 – learn how to produce graphics that influence rather than confuse. This chapter is especially good if you hate Excel.

## Consider this

Nudge is all around us. You'll feel it in your figures and your toes. The next time you're at the doctors or dentists, search for examples on nudge on posters and notices. It's everywhere in medicine, as the nudgers get us to give up smoking and check our bits for lumps.

# Chapter 10

# Finding your writing voice

The last time I was here in Margate Rocks was the mid-90s, when a fight broke out between some rockers and a gang of local drug dealers. The place was derelict for many years and was occasionally hit by *Margate lightning*, which is local slang for arson.

It's very different now. A consortium of cash-rich Londoners bought the place, stripped out the plastic chairs and furnished it with retro Formica. The humble coffee bar now has its own Instagram account.

This place is great for people watching. Take Jez. He's shouting down his phone as he bangs open the door, talking so loudly that people look up from their rare-breed sausage sandwiches and raise eyebrows at their neighbours. Jez keeps his phone jammed to his ear as he barks out his order to Aimee the barista. 'Double shot, no sugar. To go. Need it now!'

Jez snatches back his mobi and bumps into Pete as he rushes out through the door. Pete shakes the sand off his trainers before entering. He waves to a couple of people he knows and blows a kiss towards a woman with sleeve tattoos stretching up both arms. He smiles at the barista. 'How's tricks, Aimee?'

'Not bad at all', she says. 'Loving this weather'. The sun has just broken through the clouds. They both stare at rays which stream through the café's window.

'What can I get you, Pete?'

'The usual please'.

You've already formed different opinions of the two customers, even though all they've done is speak a couple of sentences and order a drink.

Jez is rude, self-centred, uncaring but also dynamic, direct and busy.

Pete is friendly, charming, open to others but also slow, too casual, perhaps a man with too much time on his hands.

The way people speak tells us a lot about them. We judge a person's voice – friendly, pompous, aggressive, submissive – to be a guide to their character. It's the same with companies. We believe a company's voice represents what a company offers.

DOI: 10.4324/9781003513520-13

## What's a writing voice?

The right voice breathes life into your company, making it as human and as recognisable as a friend. It connects with potential customers even before they know what you're selling.

One way into this is to visualise your company as a person. Do you see a gender, an age, a style of clothing, a haircut? If not, focus harder. Are they indoors or outside, sitting at a desk or jumping out of a plane? If you get stuck, imagine them as part of an ensemble cast. Who would they be in *Stranger Things* or *Modern Family*? Are they more likely to appear in *The Simpsons* than *The Sopranos*? Which one of the *Friends* are they most like?

Social media studies prove that customers will happily share posts if they find them interesting, funny or wise. They're far less likely to tweet your discount vouchers or details of your payment plan. They want to share emotional connections, not information. The right voice makes them feel they're sharing the words of a friend or a trusted advisor, not a profit-gouging corporation. Concentrate on using your voice to connect rather than to sell.

Your voice has to communicate your character from the first click. All the factors we talked about in Part 2 – word choice, sentence construction, paragraph length – tell people who you are.

## What's brand voice?

So far I've avoided the over-used phrase *brand voice*, but I can't put off the inevitable any longer. A brand voice is the tone you use when you're speaking to your clients. Brand voice can be as different as the letters sent by tax authorities to late payers (cold, analytical, threatening) and the posters advertising this summer's swimming camp (enthusiastic, welcoming, light-hearted).

Successful companies are hyper-aware of who's reading their writing. How do they want to be spoken to? Do they see the company as a long-term friend, a reliable problem-solver who helped them in the past, or someone new and exciting who arouses their curiosity? The voice you choose must reflect their wishes.

A winning brand voice is unique. Existing customers should be able to tell the email is from you just by the way it's been written. That's why companies that try to imitate successful brand voices – the supportive and positive Dove or the friendly and direct MailChimp – always come across as inauthentic and unoriginal. What you represent (the finest sausages in the market, the most healing ayurvedic treatments in Goa) must be reflected in your voice. Are you about value for money, environmental sustainability, luxury, reliability or taking a risk with something new? Really great companies express their uniqueness through their voice.

Diesel Jeans are from Italy, but they're not about heritage and tradition like so many Italian brands. Their *Be Stupid* campaign told buyers they were daring and bold. The language was deliberately blunt – *smart might have the brains, but stupid has the balls.*

If Diesel is naughtiness, Harley Davidson is rebellion. Its vocabulary – *All for freedom, freedom for all* – encourages potential buyers to get into touch with their inner outlaw Oatly – far more cuddly than Harley, but also kooky – share their voice with your friend's weird sister, the one who always smells of hash. You know it straight from the first line of their website. *Cookies go nicely with oat drinks. As it happens, the digital kind do too. So is it okay with you if we use cookies on this site?* Friendly, polite, silly, different.

## Why brand voice matters

1. Your company stands out. Many professional service firms look more or less the same to potential clients. If you found your lawyer, surveyor or accountant online, it's likely that voice was the only factor that made it stand out from its competitors. The right voice 'speaks' to people.

2. Your company becomes a person. Think back to Jez and Pete in the coffee bar. I deliberately avoided telling you any of their physical characteristics and you don't know what they're wearing other than Pete's got trainers on today. But your mind, without you even noticing, has made an image of them. The same happens when people interact with a company, especially over a long time. Voice makes a company human and creates a bond that's less about price and more about emotional connection.

3. You tell your customers who you are. Perhaps you're the friendly guys who cut down branches in spring or the dynamic and slightly crazed personal trainer who's going to make them sweat 750 calories in a 45-minute session. Perhaps you're the yoga teacher who's all about the spiritual journey or maybe you're the authoritative dietician who's got the glucose stats at her fingertips.

## Want do readers want from a brand voice?

They love consistency. They don't trust a brand that's serious and staid on Facebook, yet fun and flirty on Twitter. It shouldn't matter that your social media was written by four people in three different departments but it has to read like it has come from a single source. No-one wants a sudden outbreak of rules and regulations in the middle of a flyer announcing a pub crawl round Budapest, just like no-one wants jokes in a message announcing that 25% of the workforce is about to be made redundant.

I don't want to teach through negative examples, but sometimes you have to know what to avoid. Here's a list I sent to a friend of mine who had just opened an Etsy selling second-hand Omega watches. Although she was after help for a startup, these ideas apply to big companies as well:

1. Be careful about imposing a brand voice when none exists. If you're starting a new venture, allow yourself time to develop the writing style that fits you.
2. Find a brand voice that matches you, the individual. If your website is formal, yet you're relaxed and casual, you'll create a disconnect in people's minds. They might sense you aren't authentic, and that's never been one of your objectives, has it?
3. Don't bring in the consultants too early, or you'll end up sounding like the rest of their clients. You need some reflexion – and plenty of time listening to your first clients – before you set your voice rules.
4. Slang is a great way to make you seem hip and groovy and also a great way to make you seem out of date and out of touch. Slang dates very quickly, so make sure you check with a young person what they understand by *flex*, *cheugy*, *peng* or *salty*.[1]

### How to change your tone of voice

Remember the last time someone said to you *I don't like your tone of voice?* It was a sure sign that something was wrong in your communication – you were a teenager arguing with your teacher, or an annual review was going very badly indeed.

A quick distinction before we march on. Your company's voice is shown by the adjectives people use to describe it – *professional, friendly, inspiring, hostile.* Tone changes this voice, depending on the audience you're speaking to and the channel you're using. You want one voice, which you can modify with the many different tones out there.[2]

By my reckoning there are three common factors that change your tone of voice. I'll explain each one with a couple of examples. Always keep in mind that your readers bring different perceptions to your writing. What may be slightly too formal for one of them may be slightly too informal for another. But this isn't a reason to give up! The more you consciously work on these three factors, the more you'll make the impact you want.

| What you can change | |
|---|---|
| Formal | Informal |
| Serious | Funny |
| Matter of fact | Emotional |

### Formal/informal

This is such a tricky area. Being formal can communicate authority, knowledge and a sense of control over the situation. But it can also make you seem stiff, stuffy and old-fashioned. But being too informal is also risky. I once saw an advert for a doctor that featured him juggling stethoscopes as he outlined different treatments for heart murmurs. I gave him a miss.

You can make your writing more informal by using contractions. The meaning of *I will not play that song* and *I won't play that song* are the same, but the tone is very different. Any contraction – *don't* for *do not*, *isn't* for *is not* – is always a move towards informality. Be sensitive about the subject matter before you contract words. If it's a press release where you want to sound like you're talking to a mate, then please swap *it is* for *it's*. But if it is a formal notice about the resolution of a long-running legal dispute, do not use the contracted form as it may jar with the reader.

Salutations also indicate changes in formality. When we write to people we don't know we tend to begin with *Dear Anna* and then something along the lines of *I would like to introduce my company*. Our sign-offs are similarly formal – *with kindest regards* and *respectfully yours*. But the change towards informality in emails is very rapid, and we're soon writing *Hi Anna* and *speak soon*. Be careful if your recipient returns to formal language after a period of informality. That's often a sign that you've been too informal or that the relationship is cooling.

### Serious/funny

What do you choose? That depends on who you are and what you do. Attempts at humour and informality from an investment fund rarely work well with clients. *Oopsie doopsie, we've just lost all your dosh* isn't the best way to tell people you've ruined their retirement. And we'd avoid any comedy club that promised *an evening of humorous anecdotes that commences promptly at 8.30 pm and terminates at precisely 10 pm*.

This isn't the right place for me to teach you how to make jokes. (*And you're not the right person*, I hear you chorus.) I advise you to trial your funny stuff with colleagues before you go public. If you get any resistance from them, re-consider your material. I'm usually in favour of people being light-hearted, but context is everything.

### Matter of fact/emotional

Most business documents used to be written in the third person (*it is to be hoped that the acquisition will be a success*), as if the writer was a scientist writing up an experiment. This style – passive, wordy, a bit head teacher – is a default mode when spreading a message that requires compliance from the reader. Use matter of fact writing to convey a message that's serious and important or for taking readers through a process. You'll come across it when booking a virus booster or applying for a drinks licence.

Thankfully, most business writing is moving away from long sentences and long words to a style that's simpler and more direct. Writing that's designed to produce an emotional response connects with the reader in a different way.

I always imagine someone writing in a *matter of fact* way to have their jaw closed, perhaps even slightly clamped together. They'll have concentration lines around the eyes and on the forehead. Their writing needs to be detailed and precise, because there's a lot at risk if they miss a step or lack clarity. The more emotional writers will have their eyes open and their eyes will zoom around the room as if searching for inspiration. They'll have drunk too much coffee.

One technique to play with here is how you refer to your company or organisation. Read the following five sentences and notice how minor changes make them sound less matter of fact.

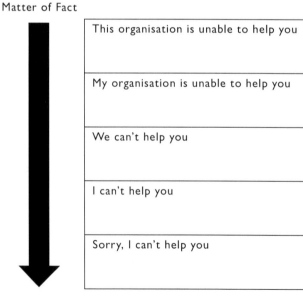

Matter of Fact

This organisation is unable to help you

My organisation is unable to help you

We can't help you

I can't help you

Sorry, I can't help you

Emotional

When people write in the third person (*this organisation*), they're aiming for a neutral, dispassionate voice. That move from *we* to *I* always signifies a style that is becoming more relaxed and personable. A single word (*sorry*) may be enough to change the reader's perception of your tone.

## Where to now?

Chapter 8 – vocabulary is the element of writing style that most affects me. I can't stand the unnecessarily formal, and I'm sceptical about people who use many complex words when one simple word will do the job.

Chapter 13 – looking to get readers on your side? Read up about how creating rapport boosts your writing charisma.

Listen to adverts. What is the tone the voiceover artist is trying to get across? Use our three categories to evaluate the tone – where does it fit in terms of *formal/informal, serious/funny* and *matter of fact/emotional.* Does the tone fit the message?

## Notes

1  I accept I'll be caught in a trap of my own making. By the time you read these words, they'll be out of date. And so will I.
2  And lots of different ways of analysing them. My three-axis approach is how I do it, but there are many different ways to split up this particular pie.

Chapter 11

# Key messages in crisis communications

Hmmmm. Your CEO has tweeted racist content (John Demsey at Esteé Lauder), your bosses in the finance department have been convicted of laundering drug money (Wachovia Bank), your staff have been posting live spiders and cockroaches to customers they don't like (eBay).

How do you write to employees, customers and suppliers about these transgressions? How can you influence what the world thinks about your company when you've clearly done something very wrong?

Crisis comms covers everything from directors not thinking the internet would be a good place to sell books (Borders) to your noodles tasting ever so slightly too much of lead (Maggi). There's always a lot at stake with crisis comms. Employees leave the firm, and customers shun its products. The share price collapses and a brand is destroyed.

## Crisis comms has three aims

A well-prepared firm minimises damage by being open with everyone – victims,[1] customers, staff, stakeholders, the media, SM. People – even those who have no connection to the crisis – are going to judge your written comms. These may be the most sensitive (and vital) words you'll ever need to write.

I've worked with several companies during the crisis phase. Whilst every disaster is different, successful communicators always have these three objectives in common.

### 1. They want to share verified information as quickly as they can

You don't have to know everything to communicate effectively. In the very early stages, any message is better than silence

Should people stop using your babyfood because it's contaminated, or should they avoid your shop downtown because of the fire? Speed is of

DOI: 10.4324/9781003513520-14

the essence. Some phrases to use now include *we want to make sure you have the most up-to-date information* and *we will provide you with regular updates as we learn more*.

Poor communication can be fatal. The CEO of SVB, Greg Becker, issued this message following a loss made by the bank on its bond portfolio and the collapse of a client. *My ask is just to stay calm, because that's what's important.*

The message – which was late, authoritarian and lacking in details – was a disaster. When you ask people to be calm, they always assume that there's a reason for them to panic! The tone and word choice of the message created the exact opposite of what Becker wanted. Spooked, depositors pulled their money as fast as they could. Becker's poor crisis comms torpedoed SVB, creating the very bank crash that he had hoped to avoid.

### 2. They want to reassure people who are worried and afraid

A crisis creates uncertainty, doubt, confusion and – on occasions – sheer terror. It's your job to reassure people. They want empathy, action and accuracy.

Empathy – a simple *we are sorry for the inconvenience this will inevitably cause you* — shows that you understand what people are going through. It's good to use *we* and *us* because you're in it together. Empathetic phrases – *we understand, we appreciate, we acknowledge* – work well.

When a passenger on a Southwest Airlines's flight died after an engine malfunction, the company's CEO, Gary Kelly, immediately responded with a heartfelt apology. Here are some extracts from the email Southwest sent to customers the day after the death.

> We value you as our customer and hope you will allow us another opportunity to restore your confidence in Southwest as the airline you can count on for your travel needs.

> In this spirit, we are sending you a check to cover any of your immediate financial needs.

> Our primary focus and commitment is to assist you in every way possible.

Why does this work? First up, it's a quick response. Secondly, the tone is authentic – the phrase *in this spirit* is high in empathy. The compensation is immediate and made without argument. No-one wants to be nickel-and-dimed when they've just witnessed a fellow passenger die.

Action shows you are doing something to right the situation. Lead off with phrases like *we're putting appropriate measures in place, we're taking immediate action* and, if appropriate, *we're now working closely with the emergency services.*

What you leave out is as important as what you put in. Don't refer to rumours or speculation, don't attempt to pass the buck, don't seek to avoid your responsibility.

Base your response on the journalistic classic of the 5Ws – when, where, who, what, why. Information may be limited, but the more verified details you can give, the better for everyone involved.

### 3. They want to ensure their organisation is seen as trustworthy

Let's face facts. A crisis is never good news for a company. But a company can make it worse with poor messaging or – worst of all – an attitude of no comment. You never want *case escalation*, where your response becomes a bigger story than the original event.

In 2018 customers were directed away from the British Airways (BA) website to a fake website. Personal and credit card details of 380,000 customers were stolen. The media broadcast news of the cyberattack before BA contacted its customers, and the airline was heavily criticised for the ponderous way the crisis was communicated. The reputational damage was huge, as was BA's fine.

## Comms and corporate integrity

I always feel uncomfortable when a firm promises me something and doesn't deliver. That gap – between what a firm says and what it does – is also noticed by staff. When they begin to doubt the integrity of their leaders and colleagues, systemic mistrust is created. Very few firms will prosper in this environment.

One of my favourite Greek proverbs states that *a fish rots from its head*. It's the leaders who create the culture of a firm, and if they are dishonest, that will filter through to all levels of the organisation. This obviously applies to large-scale fraud and corruption but it also shows up in much smaller incidents – lying to a customer about a delivery date or not honouring a discount.

Let me show you the importance of organisation integrity with a negative example.

The NRA is a lobbying organisation which promotes wider ownership of guns in the United States. It's issued a lengthy and wordy *Statement of Corporate Ethics* which includes the below line:

No Association employee shall engage in illegal or unethical actions involving any person or organization doing business or attempting to do business with the Association.

But the NRA has been beset by accusations of corruption, deceit and incitement to violence for many decades. In 2024, for example, its chairman was fined $4.4 million for spending the organisation's funds on personal flights, luxury vacations and entertainment. Statements of values, mission statements and ethics manuals are meaningless in corrupt organisations.

## Where to now?

Chapter 10 – flip back and consider how brand voice needs to change when an organisation has to reassure staff, protect customers from a dangerous product and limit damage to its reputation.

Chapter 15 – crisis comms might well be the most important messages you ever send. You will become aware of a trade-off between accuracy and speed. Make sure you edit and revise with care. And please get someone else to proof the message, no matter how urgent.

## Try this

At least one company is facing a new crisis today. Go online, and find the crisis communications, and then track how they change over time. See if you can identify the *point of reassurance*, when the company believes that the disaster is over and the world can return to business as usual.

## Note

1  Yeah, I know, a loaded word. Before you get all judgemental, why not send me your alternative? I'm all ears.

# Chapter 12

# The six bricks of an unbeatable argument

Imagine you have 250 words to convince a reader. That's more or less the length of this page. You've learned a lot about *how* to get your message across in the previous 11 chapters, but for the moment, I want you to concentrate on *what* you need to show.

The six bricks approach uses a variety of strategies to make its impact. It's also a fantastic way to refine your thoughts. Once you can fill each brick with a strong sentence, you'll know you have control over your subject. And that's going to help you tremendously to articulate your thoughts with skill and authority.

## The hook

This is how you grab the attention of the reader. Look for a surprising example, an original quote, a rhetorical question that makes people stop and think. Freshness beats clickbaiting every time.

*I see the person I'm talking to as I write.*

## Your contention

Your view, which states your position on the hook. (You'll know this as your *thesis statement* if you've got an academic background.)

*The more you focus on a single reader, the more your writing connects with many different people.*

## Your credibility

Readers want to know why they should read you. Make it clear that you have sufficient experience and education to present a worthwhile argument.

*I've taught writing all over the world to many different types of people.*

DOI: 10.4324/9781003513520-15

## Your connection

Show how you conquered obstacles and achieved success. Show you are human by sharing your emotions.

*Most of us get anxious and blocked when writing at work.*

## Your evidence

What proof do you have to back up your assertions? In a world full of ill-informed big mouths, show people how your ideas have been formed.

*Your mouth is watering and your whole body is expectant. Reading this has made your mouth water, hasn't it?*

## The strong finish

Drive your argument home. More than a conclusion, this should be an energetic restatement of your main point.

*There is a kinder, gentler, and funnier way to improve your writing. And you're reading it now.*

There's a logical flow to the six bricks. Change the order at your peril, and don't ever lose a brick! I'm not going to use clumsy metaphors about weak foundations and wobbly structures, but your readers will feel something is missing.

No *Hook.* Readers aren't interested or involved.
No *Contention.* Readers have no idea where you're going with this.
No *Credibility.* Readers doubt your right to influence them.
No *Connection.* Readers don't feel the impact of your words.
No *Evidence.* Readers doubt the truth of your ideas.
No *Strong Finish.* Readers forget you and your ideas.

## The rebuttal

There's a seventh brick to consider. A rebuttal is a point which is *against* your main argument. Introducing a negative is a great way to show you are open-minded and can see the problems that detract from your proposed solution. A rebuttal creates feelings of empathy and rapport in a reader's mind – *he's being honest about what he proposes* is a compliment rather than a complaint.

Here's a structural tip that helps you slip in some negatives. It relies on two simple facts about how our memory works.

## Primacy effect – people remember what they see first

Recency Effect – people remember what they've just seen.[1]

If you've ever sat on an interview panel, judged an amateur dramatics competition or watched *X Factor*, you'll know how primacy and recency work. You remember the first and last person, but people in the middle tend to fade away.

People are more convinced by the information they receive first, and they also tend to remember a big finish. A message presented in the middle of these two poles is likely to be lost. Consider the adverts they play in the cinema before you watch a movie. You remember the first one and the last one, but you pay more attention to your popcorn than the ads in the middle. Our recall of first and last impressions is strong.

Use these tendencies to your advantage. Start with your strongest idea, and end with an idea or example that's powerful. Mention the negative in the middle because your listeners will remember the trust you created but are likely to forget the actual point that you made.

Phrases like *first the really big news* and *you'll love this new idea* in teaser campaigns use primacy for their impact. Reminder messages – *our annual subscription package saves you ten per cent, Duolingo has missed you* – are all about recency.

## How to instantly weaken your argument

After the positive example of the six bricks, it's only fair to warn you about approaches that will damage your reputation. Don't resort to these six fallacies in your writing, because they make you appear petty, ill-informed, biased and even crazed. And these, I hope, are not attributes that you want attached to your work.

You'll see examples in the comments section below any controversial article. In some ways, this is a good thing. Subjects that are complex – gun control in the United States, democracy in Russia – are never easy to solve. It's a fair bet that a discussion that's been running for decades, or even centuries, has good arguments on both sides. But most of the comments we are going to consider are dumb trolls attacks, rather than coherent additions to the debate.

## The false dichotomy

This occurs when people present a decision as binary. *We either sell our Headquarters or we don't.* The best solution may reside in a grey area – we could rent out two floors, or use the Headquarters for other purposes. As soon as someone comes up with a third choice, the false dichotomy makes you look dogmatic and inflexible.

## Bandwagon jumping

Recommending a course of action just because lots of other people are doing it isn't a great idea. The Great Financial Crisis of 2007 and 2008 had its roots in banks copying other banks in granting mortgages to too many sub-prime customers at the same time. Interest rates spiked suddenly, and many borrowers were unable to pay the monthly interest.

## Appealing to tradition

We take comfort from the past. *We've always used them to supply our ice cream, and I see no reason to switch now.* But this approach betrays a reluctance to change and look for better options.

## The hasty conclusion

This happens when someone investigates a very small sample of people, cases or companies and draws the wrong conclusion. If you want to improve customer service, there's no point telling the anecdote about the one customer who always rates you five out of five.

## The expert from another field

This is extremely common on TV and radio. I can understand why someone who's really good at outdoor survival presents a programme on, say, birdwatching. But I don't see why they should then be interviewed about their opinion of NATO. Be careful of relying on the words of experts who know nothing about the topic in hand.

## *Ad Hominem* attack

This is where you attack a person simply because you don't like them or their cause. You're better than that, so stop if you notice yourself going down this route.

## Where to now?

Chapter 7 – learn how the SCQA introduction grabs readers' attention.
   Chapter 15 – storytelling creates a bond with your readers. How do great storytellers show concepts like credibility, connection and evidence?

The comments section of local papers is often a rich source of poor reasoning. Dive in, and see if you can find examples of spurious appeals to tradition and attacks. (Sadly, you won't have to search too hard.) Notice how your opinion of the commenter worsens with each weak argument.

## Note

1 These are the correct terms for what we saw in Chapter 9, when Beatrice told me that customers only remember the first two and last items on a menu.

# Part 4

## Charisma

### A Better Way to Make an Impact

# Chapter 13

# A beginner's guide to charisma

We all know when we meet someone who is charismatic.

They radiate a graceful power, an authority that comes from experience and wisdom rather than from arrogance and pomposity. They show their interest in the people they lead. Not in that distracted, struggling-for-a-question way which marked the late Prince Philip's royal visits, but with authenticity and charm and genuine human warmth. Above all else they have presence. Wherever they are – in a one-to-one meeting, or approaching the mike in a 60,000-seater stadium – they are the person we want to be with.

Your challenge is to get across these wonderful charismatic qualities – authority, empathy, presence – in your writing. What's at stake? Your teams will work better, you'll get people to follow you, readers will commit to you in small and large ways and you, my friend, will be a writer of influence.

## The language of rapport

Rapport is a feeling of harmony with another person. You experience rapport when you know your team mate trusts you, or when you're sure the boss will support your latest proposal. Rapport is that laugh you share over a cocktail after you've survived a howling mistake with a client.

Sometimes rapport is instant and spontaneous. We just hit it off with someone, and we don't need to analyse why. But it's more usual, especially at work, for rapport to build up over time. Rapport needs empathy, an understanding of the feelings of others, to flourish.

Writing to one specific person can make us super nervous. That request for an appraisal, rejecting a great candidate for a job, the customised sales letter to the wealthiest potential client you've ever met. What will distinguish you from the also-rans is the quality of your language.

Building rapport through email is a difficult task. But the person you're talking to – and I do say *talking to* even though you're writing to

DOI: 10.4324/9781003513520-17

them – will give you clues along the way. Read carefully, and they'll show you how they want you to communicate with them. Your choice of words and phrases will determine if you make a connection, or if you are just another contender who doesn't quite fit the bill.

But first, a trip to the movies.

## What *The Silence of the Lambs* tells us about empathy

That's not a headline I ever thought I'd write, but Jonathan Demme's thriller is a masterclass in how to produce empathy. From the first seconds, while the opening credits are still running and you're settling into your seat, the director creates a bond between the hero of his story and the audience. It means we care for her and experience the same highs and terrifying, horrific, heart-pumping lows as she does.

Let's take a look at the opening scene. A young woman is running through the forest. She pulls hard on a rope as she climbs a muddy track. She's out of breath but super determined. A man shouts out her name.

WOODS NEAR QUANTICO, VA
*FBI AGENT*:  Starling! Starling!

Always pay attention to what name a novelist or scriptwriter gives to a character. Starling? A defenceless, tiny bird that's easy prey for a much stronger predator. Our minds make a connection with the flapping of a bird we hear in the background.

*FBI AGENT*:  Crawford wants to see you in his office.
*STARLING*:  Thank you, sir.

We sense that Clarice Starling is different, that she doesn't quite fit in. She's alone as she passes groups of other FBI students. She's friendly (she gets a high five from a friend) but she's not the sort of person who stops for a chat. The FBI building is a modern, institutional, block and Starling looks a little too colourful to fit in. She's always going against the traffic, always walking against the flow of other people, which is something all of us have felt at one time or another.

Clarice steps into a lift full of men. All of them are at least a head taller than her, and all of them wear the FBI uniform of red polo shirt, chinos and name badge. She's tiny, female, dressed differently, alone.

The exit from the lift is crucial. Looking around the Behavioural Science Services unit we spot clues – pictures on a wall, the word *skins* written on a blackboard – that suggest something very bad is about to be revealed. She's in the world of adults now, no longer part of the student cohort. Most of us can remember a moment when we were selected to do something different, something unexpected. It's exciting and frightening at the same time.

But Crawford isn't in his office. We beg Starling not to turn around, not to look at the pictures on his walls, not to get involved. But too late. We look at the wall, with its horrific images of torture and bloodshed, but we're now the same height as Starling.

Why do we have so much empathy with Starling? Empathy occurs because we can see the world from the point of view of another person. We see Starling's life through her eyes, not our own. We can imagine what it feels like to face her predicament, because all of us have struggled to achieve a goal, been out of our depth, been terrified by a challenge. When Agent Starling finally battles the real villain of the film, we cheer for her.

---

### Being caring is a strength, not a weakness

Some people confuse empathy with weakness. These are the people who don't lead their team but *whip them into shape*. They regard emotions as a barrier to their objectives and have a tendency to dismiss the concerns of others as irrelevant or even stupid. Bullying and frightening people are poor long-term strategies if you want to become a great communicator.

---

### Senses tells us a lot about people

What phrases do people use when they feel rapport? *We're on the same wavelength, he's got my back, she sees the world like I do.* Be alert to how people sign off their emails because you can often get a clue from the last line. *Let's touch base, we can arrive at an agreement, I hope you can see an answer to our problem.* All these clues give away the language they prefer to use.

These phrases all come from the senses. Auditory people are likely to write *I hear you* or ask you to *tell me more*, while the more visual amongst us will *change their point of view* or complain they can't *see what you mean*. Someone who is primarily kinaesthetic is all about touch and movement, so they will *grasp your point*. A client with a strong sense of smell will tell you *the pricing smells off* or *the proposal stinks*.

Foodie types are especially fascinating. A teacher may ask you to *digest a book*, even if it's very *meaty*, before you *regurgitate* its contents for an exam. Your answer may be *half-baked* or a little *raw*, or *not to their taste*. You can *sink your teeth* into a novel, even if the ending is *hard to stomach*. Choosing the right words has an enormous impact on your ability to build rapport. I guess that's the major *takeaway* from this chapter.[1]

So pay attention to the words people write. The upcoming table lists a few examples but there are many more that people use. Now you've got the idea, you'll notice them all the time. To make all our lives easier, I've lumped in the smell and taste people under kinaesthetic.

*Table 13.1 Three types of people and the language they use*

|  | Visual people | Auditory people | Kinaesthetic people |
|---|---|---|---|
| This is how they agree with you | I see what you mean | I hear what you're saying | It feels right to me |
|  | It's clear to me | That sounds perfect | Your proposal is a good fit |
|  | I've got a full picture now | It chimes with us | It should lead to a positive impact |
| These are the verbs they use | Let's focus on this | We can talk this over | Do get in touch |
|  | Can you clarify this point? | Can you tell me more? | We can firm up the details later |
|  | I see your point of view | I'm sorry to hear that | How do we move on from this? |
| These phrases give you clues | I look forward to seeing you | It's been a harmonious process | What impact did that have? |
|  | How do you see that happening? | It's music to my ears | She's a bitter individual |
|  | The future looks hazy/bright | I listened to my heart | Take the rough with the smooth |

## How to use this new-found knowledge

I don't advise you to parrot the vocabulary of the person you're communicating with. But I do encourage you to pay close attention to phrases they use which hint at a sensory preference. Then you can pepper your writing to gustatory types with the odd foodie phrase or make your words chime with auditory people. Try it, and your one-to-one written communication will become much more effective.

Don't worry if a word *isn't in harmony* with you or a phrase *just feels wrong*. That's just your personal preference *speaking to you*. Your challenge is to *put to one side* your preferred mode of expression as you *focus on* what your reader wants *to hear*. And, you'll be *relieved* to know that's quite enough italic for this paragraph.

## Four more simple ways to build rapport in your emails

In difficult situations, it's especially important to consciously work on rapport. You could be HR telling off Jez[2] for his heinous behaviour at the sales conference. Or you could be Jez begging HR for forgiveness for his unfortunate lapse of judgement at the sales conference. In either case, there are some linguistic approaches that can make the process less painful.

1. Pronouns are us. Empathetic writers use *we* and *us*, rather than *me/I* or *the company/this organisation*.
2. The language of support. Words like *help, together* and *jointly* show you're an *empath* (which is a great word I didn't know existed before I wrote this chapter). You might also consider slipping in *cooperation, side by side* and *reasonable*.
3. Use the conditional form. Beginning sentences with *if we work together on this* will create more of a bond than *there's only one way to do this – my way*.
4. Words of encouragement. These show that you care about the reader and you want to open up a dialogue. Phrases like *Tell me your opinion* and *I'm interested in what you think* foster a spirit of collaboration.

## Where to now?

To follow up these themes, go to:

Chapter 8 – it's all about word choice, isn't it? The techniques in our current chapter are best applied to one-to-one communication, but do try and get the senses involved in all your writing. What is the taste and smell and touch of a Burberry raincoat, a Cathay Pacific flight or a night out in Dubai?

Chapter 9 – return to our chapter on persuasion. Can you see how using tailored language will lead to mutual understanding and, as a result, more effective writing?

Do this. Think about three of your favourite novels that are narrated by the hero. You probably won't remember most of the plot, but I bet you'll remember their voice and how it connected with you. Three wonderful first-person novels I can recommend are *The Great Gatsby* by F. Scott Fitzgerald, *The Bell Jar* by Sylvia Plath and *The Colour Purple* by Alice Walker.

## Notes

1 BTW, the posh adjective for the sense of smell is *olfactory*, and it's *gustatory* for the sense of taste.
2 That's Jez from Margate Rocks in Chapter 10, if you've been paying attention.

# Chapter 14

# The quest for clarity

## Make your words concrete

Being detailed and specific will turn you into a more effective writer. Read any novel about personal struggle – Cormac McCarthy's *The Road* is my current book – and you'll see that the more personal and specific the details of the adversity, the greater the connection you feel with the main character. The right language creates immediate impact. Abstract words and generic phrases just leave readers cold.

I've been sent a brochure from a sales-training company. There's nothing terrible about their writing, but they're not getting enough people to sign up to their seminars. They've asked me for a rewrite. Let me talk you through the changes I made to this single line:

> *The program will provide delegates with opportunities to rehearse real-life situations.*

The improvements I suggested are relatively simple. They are all designed to create a clearer picture in the reader's mind.

*Program* – to me this conjures up the image of a piece of paper (an outline for a course) rather than a classroom where people learn.
*Will* – the use of the future tense makes the image more vague. Putting it in the present tense sharpens the definition.
*Delegates* – a bland, corporate word. I see bored people in formal business wear struggling to make chit-chat outside a bleak breakout room. Far better to appeal directly to the readers with *you*.
*The program will* – whatever comes first in a sentence is most prominent in reader's minds. The original word order placed more emphasis on the program than the attendees. I change the order to put *you* first.
*Opportunities* – we don't need this word. I want this sentence to work hard, so I cut anything superfluous.

DOI: 10.4324/9781003513520-18

*Rehearse* – I automatically think of acting and pretending to have a role. I want something more precise. It's a marginal change, but I go for *practise*

*Real-life situations* – so vague that it doesn't produce any image in my mind.

Once I change these words, edit them and jiggle about with the order, I end up with a sentence that's shorter, punchier, more concrete and much more effective in getting bums on their seats.

*You practise pitching to a client on the course.*

## Show the details

We all slip too easily into abstractions when writing. We're tempted to use bland words like *results, innovation, solution, flexible* and *intelligent* because we read them all the time in the corporate world. But these words lack impact. Your eyes glaze over every time a writer uses *empower, actionable* or *deliverable*. So don't!

Good business writers believe in the maxim *show, don't sell*. They use word choice, metaphors and specific examples to be concrete. Details move people, while generalities put them in a coma.

Here are some examples of how to move from the vague and abstract to the detailed and concrete.

*Table 14.1 Choose words that turn abstract into concrete*

| Abstract idea | Made concrete by |
| --- | --- |
| We offer a fast and reliable delivery service | 99% of our deliveries arrive within 30 minutes |
| The company offers students a wide variety of pre-recorded materials | We're the Netflix of education |
| I am a very experienced project manager who has worked on complex projects | I project managed the merger between Trinity and Blackstone |
| Our software helps you achieve your goals | Our software doubles your leads |
| Our casual shoes are available in a range of attractive colours | You can buy our sneakers in red, green or yellow |

## Take responsibility for your writing

Take a look at this text from a BP ad, which details their response to the Deepwater Horizon oil disaster. The impact of the blowout was terrible:

11 people died in the explosion, marine life was destroyed for generations, fishing and tourism were badly hit.

*The Gulf oil spill is a tragedy that never should have happened.*
*And while we were deeply disappointed that the recent 'top kill' operation was unsuccessful, we were also prepared. The best engineers in the world are now working around the clock to contain and collect most of the leak. As they do that, BP will continue to take full responsibility for cleaning up the spill.*

BP's word choices are deliberate. A *spill* is what happens when your cup wobbles in a saucer – it's small and easily contained. It's an odd way to describe a mistake so large that it would eventually cost BP $60 billion in fines, restitution and clean-up costs. We typically use *tragedy* when describing events that are out of our control, like earthquakes and avalanches. We use *accident* or *disaster* to describe events that are caused by humans – *air traffic accident, the Aberfan colliery disaster of 1966*. It's a subtle distinction, but *tragedy* hints at an act of god, rather than corporate greed.

The phrase *never should have happened* is the closest BP get to an apology. But the language and grammar distance BP from admitting responsibility for the disaster. It's a world away from saying *we caused this disaster*. The company's slogans are big and bold – *We will get it done. We will make it right* – but there's no concrete detail of what BP is actually doing. And did you notice the way BP slip in *most* in the final sentence of the second paragraph? Our expectations are most definitely being managed.

How do you feel as you wade through BP's faux-apology? Lied to, manipulated, tricked? The negative emotions you feel about this writing will become associated with BP. They strike us as arrogant, condescending and dishonest.

### Your choices of words and grammar affect processing

A bit of jargon for you. Unclear writing reduces your reader's *processing fluency*, which measures how quickly and easily they understand you. Clearer writing leads to faster processing, which leads to a positive reaction towards your writing style from the reader. Readers are always amenable to a message they can process quickly.

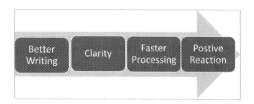

*Figure 14.1*

Thankfully, there are many writing techniques that speed up a reader's processing fluency. Here are five of them.

### 1. Choose the active over the passive

This is the difference between:

Active – *I enjoy this book*
Passive – *The book is being enjoyed by me*

The passive form inverts the active order of Subject (I), Verb (enjoy), Object (this book) into Object, Verb, Subject (the book is enjoyed by me). The passive always uses more words and the grammatical structure is more complex. This requires more processing by the reader, which will weaken your impact.

The passive also reduces your authority as a writer (and as a human) because it gives the impression that you don't want to accept responsibility. A child will say to an irate parent *the plate was broken* rather than *I broke the plate*. If that child grows up to be a politician, they'll use the passive to distance themselves from problems and bad news.

There's a big difference in emphasis between *regeneration was delayed by the councillor's lack of leadership* and *the councillor's lack of leadership delayed regeneration*. The first version passes (or at least hides) the buck while the second clearly shows who has caused the delay.

### 2. Use positive language

The original title of the section you've just read was *avoid the passive tense*. I changed it because I wanted my reader to make a positive decision *(choose)* rather than a negative *(avoid)*. The positive always has a greater impact, so that's why saying *remember to check your tickets* gets a better response from passengers than *don't forget to check your tickets*.

A similar concept is in play when you look at ads for gyms. Humans get more motivated by gains than losses. While *losing weight* may be your primary aim, you're far more likely to take out a membership at a place that promises you'll *gain the perfect body*.

Here are some more examples of how to turn negative language into positive.

### 3. Vary your words

Repetition is the enemy of concentration. Every language has synonyms which you can use. I'm not advising you to replace *office cleaner* with *workspace amelioration officer*. This is about adding variety, not complexity.

*Table 14.2 Replace negative language with positive*

| Negative | Replace with positive |
|---|---|
| You can't use the main door today while the garden is being dug | You can use the side door today while the garden is being dug |
| Sorry, we can't refund the cost of your therapy until you send us the authorised invoice | Send us the authorised invoice so we can refund the cost of your therapy |
| Please don't run in the corridor | Please walk in the corridor |
| Our refurbishment won't disrupt the smooth running of your office | Our refurbishment fits perfectly around your office routine |
| Don't be negative! | Be positive! |

Here's 56 words of random text from an Australian business paper.

*Australian testimonial software provider Vouch wants rapid staff recruitment after raising $8 million in a funding round. The oversubscribed funding round also raised money from angel investors for the testimonial software provider, with the funding to go toward the development of new features and doubling the company's staff of 20 both in Australia and the US.*

We make this less repetitious by employing some imaginative synonyms

*Australia/Australian* – make the first one *Sydney-based*
*Testimonial software provider* – change the second one to *the company* or, better still, *start-up*.
*Funding round* – changed the first one to *new investment*, but you could quibble and say the *new* isn't needed. And I changed *funding* to *money*.
*Raising/raised* – I'll try *attracted*
*Staff* – change the second one to *headcount*

*Sydney-based testimonial software provider Vouch wants rapid staff recruitment after raising $8 million in new investment. The funding round also raised money from angel investors for the start-up, with the money to go toward the development of new features and doubling the company's staff of 20 both in Australia and in the United States.*

All other things being equal, a great variety makes for an easier read.

One twist on this is when you're referring to someone in an email. It's more polite to use a person's name twice before switching to she, he or they. So I follow *Shane is an excellent choice* with *Let's check Shane's availability* rather than *Shane is an excellent choice. Let's check her availability.*

This is especially true if Shane is copied in, because no-one likes being referred to by a third-person pronoun when they're in the conversation.

### 4. Make your numbers concrete too

Percentages are difficult to visualise for non-mathematicians. Which of these two statements have the most impact on you?

a. 90% of people prefer the presumed consent approach to organ donation
b. Nine out of ten people prefer the presumed consent approach to organ donation

In the second version, you can see the people ticking a box on a questionnaire or talking around a table at a focus group. The first version is mathematically the same but doesn't 'land' in our minds.

### 5. Throat clearing introductions

Beware of giving out information that is already obvious to the reader. If you start your email with *the purpose of this email is . . .* you've already wasted the reader's time. So avoid phrases like *this document is about . . .* and *it's my intention to inform you . . .* unless they are vital. (Which they rarely are.)

These phrases are the ums and ahs of writing. Like a speaker warming up his voice, or, er, stumbling over his first words, they give the impression that you're not quite ready to begin.

### Where to now

Chapter 2 – clear writing has its roots in clear objectives. If you get tied up, remind yourself why you're writing. Visualising a reader helps you write to them.

Chapter 6 – take a trip back to paragraphs and sentences. You'll now see that the structures we discussed are all about adding clarity. How can you use these techniques on your current writing tasks?

### Think about this

We live in a world of exhausted choice. The more cluttered your market, the more important it is to get your message across. Ikea (*Scandinavian design at a low price*) and the old-fashioned iPod (launched with 1,000 *songs in your pocket*) are great examples of simple, clear messages.

Can you describe yourself or your business in less than ten words? Give it a try.

Chapter 15

# The power of business storytelling

In my right hand I have a 40-page report entitled *Margate Bookie Funding Strategy*. In my left hand I have my phone, which is playing a one-minute video of festival highlights. What are the differences between the report and the video?

We expect the report to be full of facts and figures. It starts with an executive summary, its chapters are clearly delineated, and perhaps there's even a section full of surveys and statistics. The tone of voice will be dry and slightly stand-offish. It may change what you think about the Bookie's finances, but it won't change what you feel.

The video is all about memories. What authors were there, what did the audience look like, how chubby has the CEO got this year? Along with famous writers signing their books, you'll catch glimpses of the harbour full of suntanning novel readers. The tone of the video is light-hearted and celebratory. You'll get an impression of what a fabulous event it was, but you won't learn anything about how it's financed.

It's traditional to believe the report and the video have completely different audiences. The report gets printed off by diligent readers who highlight certain sections or cover a page with question marks. They'll read it at a big desk in a board room, and then discuss its findings at a meeting. You watch the video on your phone, while you're on the bus or waiting for your date to turn up.

But what if the report could entertain you and the video could inform you? What if the report was an experience and the video was insightful? What if there was a hybrid that combined the best of the report and the video? Welcome, my friends to business storytelling.

## The link between analysis and emotions

Skilled storytellers are experts at creating a unified audience (sometimes called a *cohort*) that thinks, acts and feels in the same way. I can still remember how the entire audience at Dreamland Cinema jumped out of their seats

DOI: 10.4324/9781003513520-19

*Figure 15.1*

when the floating head appeared in *Jaws*, and how me and my schoolmates laughed in unison at the *he ranks as high as any in Rome* line in *Life of Brian*. You'll get more buy-in from your readers when you can add some of the video elements – fun memories, positive feelings – to your message.

Reports concentrate on analytical data. My financing report includes attendee pie charts, data about ticket sales and statistics about demographics. There's supporting documentation, such as health and safety policies, and a basic cashflow. I leaven this rather stodgy mix with content that is more emotionally driven. I'll include short interviews with visiting authors, pictures of our happy audience and a poem called *Captain Poo* written by a seven-year-old environmentalist. I keep all the data, but I make its delivery more human.

Any company that helps a customer cut through the noise with a well-crafted story will always have the advantage. Customers are swamped with messages every second of their day. Buy this, sell that, swipe right, switch supplier or provider or network. You can make it easy for them to choose you by telling a story, but make sure the message is ultimately about them and not you. It's entirely possible that you make the best burgers in the barrio or that your milkshakes do actually bring all the boys to the yard. But no-one will give a damn unless you can communicate the benefits you offer to your consumers.

Too much messaging is about the company rather than customer. We don't care that your start-up has angel investors, that your new warehouse in Nicosia is state-of-the-art or that your Wall Street IPO has been a runaway success. No. We want to know how spending our cash with you will make us feel, think or act in a new way. Make you message simple. Make it human. Make it something that one happy customer can tell to another.

## What's a creation myth?

Business storytelling skills make your message connect with your audience. Don't worry; I'm not going to hit you with 50 pages of theory about the 12 stages of the hero's journey. But I am going to teach you how one type of story, the Creation Myth, can spread the message for any type of business.

The most common question for entrepreneurs is why did you start? It makes sense to have a compelling answer ready. Many corporates develop their own foundation stories. Why? They're great when you need a *capsule message*[1] for rapid communication. They're used when a founder is in full-on networking mode – spieling the elevator pitch to a venture capitalist, or recruiting talent to join the team.

Most cultures and religions in the world have a creation myth. The ancient Greeks believed that Gaia created life out of the chaos of nothingness. The Old Testament tells Christians that God created the world in six days. The Popol Vuh of the K'iche' people recounts how the inhabitants of modern-day Guatemala were initially made of earth and mud, and later of wood.

Creation myths around the world display very similar structures. They begin in a primordial state, a place of chaos and disorder. Then the gods arrive, with all their skills and special powers and a clear plan to begin life. The new world they create is, initially at least, a perfect paradise.

Now, here's the big reveal. The structure used in successful corporate foundation stories is the same as the structure used in creation myths. It's very easy to match the stages in a successful company or product launch to the five stages in a creation myth.

| | Creation Myth | Foundation Story |
|---|---|---|
| 1 | Primordial State | The market before you entered |
| 2 | New Beings | What you brought to the market |
| 3 | Conscious Creation | What convinced you there was a market |
| 4 | The Reasons for Creation | What you wanted to achieve |
| 5 | The Perfect World | Your impact on the market |

You don't believe me? Let's take a look at Fever-Tree, and how they created a product which changed a market which was long regarded as stale, mature and impossible to enter.

## The Fever-Tree Story

One of my favourite lines in advertising is their slogan – *if three quarters of your gin and tonic is the tonic, make sure you use the best*. Remember what we've said about precise numbers, personal appeal and employing the senses? It's all here. And who wouldn't want to have the best?

## We start in the primordial state

Before Fever-Tree, there were only two choices of tonic. The category killer was Schweppes, which suffered from a dowdy image. The alternative was naff own label supermarket brands, which were low quality and competed on price rather than taste. You were never going to impress a date by pouring a Vodka and Tesco.

## The new gods arrive

The late nineties saw a boom in premium spirits. An explosion in gin brands led drinkers to pay big money for artisan sprits. Stories about obscure origins and mysterious heritages proliferated, even if they were sometimes made up!

Fever-Tree spotted a big gap in the market. Consumer tastes were becoming more sophisticated, but really expensive spirits were drowned in poor-quality, artificial tasting mixers. From the first product the company launched – Indian tonic water – the emphasis was clearly on flavour rather than price. The mixer added to the taste of the drink, rather than simply diluting it.

## The gods consciously create a new world

The founders Charles Rolls and Tim Warrillow were experienced in luxury drink manufacturing and marketing, but the story they tell makes them sound like the Indiana Joneses of tonic waters. 'It really did start in the British Library, researching the history and ingredients of tonic – and then we went out to go and find them'. Part academics, part explorers, you can imagine them in pith helmets striking deals in the Democratic Republic of Congo to source tonic's vital ingredient, quinine.

Their adverts focused on ingredients that were natural, exotic and rare – fresh spices from Madagascar, bitter orange from Tanzania, green ginger from the Ivory Coast.

## The reasons for creation are clear

Our intrepid explorers used the word *hunting* instead of *purchasing* when they told people about their ingredients. Mixers – once chockfull of e-numbers and chemicals such as aspartame and saccharin – were now crafted from *botanicals*.

The competition was portrayed as staid, unsophisticated and more interested in cost cutting than the drinker's pleasure. Customers heard stories of how Fever-Tree's suppliers were actually excited to work with a company that prioritised taste. As Warrilow said, 'We told them not to worry about the price, because we just want to get the best ingredients we can'.

## The perfect world is created

The marketing team spread their foundation story to bartenders around the world, selling the tale of their mixer with the care and personal attention that was normally reserved for top end spirits. The mixer fuelled the craft gin revolution, which led to new brands and even more demand for Fever-Tree.

I'd always associated gin and tonic with England. It had a decadent, slightly louche image, something a bit naughty to take the edge off the day. So it was a surprise twist that the big break for Fever-Tree's quintessentially Anglo drink happened in Spain.

Ferran Adrià i Acosta is the three-star Michelin chef behind elBulli, once the best restaurant in the world. A G&T made from Hendrick's gin and Fever-Tree tonic became elBulli's signature drink. It was served in massive balloon glasses with lots of ice and a fair amount of fanfare. The image was priceless. A slightly fusty, old-fashioned drink was now prestigious.

Twenty years after its launch, Fever-Tree owns 28% of the total retail market for mixers. It's the most served tonic in the World's 50 Best Bars. And as I take a sip their rhubarb and raspberry mixer, I check that its stock market capitalisation is touching £2 billion. Cheers!

## Where to now?

To follow up these themes, go to:

Chapter 4 – storytelling needs a deliberate change in mindset. You're not pushing a product or service but seeking to connect with readers on an emotional level.

Chapter 10 – the appropriate writing style is vital, vital, vital for business stories. Experiment with finding a storytelling voice that suits you. Practise out loud until it feels natural to write it down. (This will take some time, especially if you're not used to this voice.)

**Think about this**

Now you're aware of this structure, you'll notice stories like this all time. Which ones can you see? Write your own, using the five steps we've outlined.

**Note**

1 I've just invented this phrase. It means *a one sentence explanation of something complicated*. Feel free to use it, royalty free.

# Chapter 16

# The human side of AI

This chapter will be out date before I finish writing it

So who knows how ancient it will be by the time you get around to reading it I'm about to sign off the final proof of this book. I'm really happy with it (of course I am!) but this particular chapter worries me. Change in this area is continuous, and it's hard to recommend technology when everything is a moving target.

Anyway, it's a sunny 24° in las Palmas. There's a 25-meter pool calling me. I'll do some laps and get my thoughts in order.

## Why am I worried about AI?

The phrase *artificial intelligence* terrifies some of us. We're petrified that not only will we lose our jobs but these damn robots are also coming to take over the planet as well. What will happen to our unique voice and our individual creativity if we subcontract it to the AI apps? And what will happen to humanity if the AI Shakespeare is better than original IRL Shakespeare?

I've got to confess that so far my experiences with AI have been mixed. I love it as a research tool, where I use it as a smart version of Google. I get it to answer requests like *give me five reasons why philanthropists choose a charity* or *what are the three most common investment strategies?*

Usually the top half of the list produced by AI is valuable. But by the time you're in the middle, there are irrelevant and incorrect results and the bottom third is – sorry to say this, AI evangelists – absolute garbage.

The big problem with AI is the quality of the writing. It's awful – bland, unmemorable, confused and boring. Is there any way I can use it, perhaps in the early stages of my writing?

## We've all used writing software in the past

I splutter out of a poorly executed tumble turn and come up for a gulp of air. I stop and ponder. What if AI is just another set of tools rather than

DOI: 10.4324/9781003513520-20

an existential threat? I've used lots of computing software over the years to make my writing easier. I make a mental list of products as I complete laps 7 and 8.

### Microsoft word

Yes, I know you've come across this before, obviously. But there's one feature I use that you might not be aware of. When you press ALT + ¬ you immediately get into text dictation. Although this isn't perfect, it may well be better than your typing and it does encourage you to 'speak your text' and keep a natural voice.

### Scrivener

If you've seen Scrivener before it's probably been in a café where some sad-faced junior novelist is bashing out their dystopian sci-fi. But hold on. Scriv (as it's known amongst the cognoscenti) is absolutely great for writing long pieces of non-fiction. The ease with which you can move around blocks of text is impressive. And its corkboard is good for planning writing tasks.

A note of warning: Scriv has lots of functionality you'll never use. Don't try to conquer it.

### Mindmapping software

I've mentioned mindmaps in Chapter 4, but there's no shame in repeating how useful they are in getting your ideas sorted. I use mindmanager, but there are lots of other similar packages available.

### Pomodoro timing apps

This is a great way to boost your word count. You set a timer for 20 minutes, then you crack on with your writing. You can't visit the bathroom or make a cup of tea, and you certainly can't go online. Your phone should be in flight mode. When your 20 minutes is up, an alarm sounds and you take a five-minute break. Repeat this three times then take a proper break. You'll write more in three Pomodoro's than you will in a day of unstructured time. There are loads of apps that do this, so I'll let you choose.

I'm on lap 13 and getting tired yet slightly philosophical. I go back to the idea that AI can be a tool to help us. I'm cautious about AI, but I've begun to employ it for what I label *zero drafts* of my writing. These are rough, rather sloppy notes that get my ideas out of my head and onto the screen.

I'm not a consistent user, but here are some ways AI has saved me time.

### Summarising my work

I use ChatGPT to cut down my work into summaries. It's quite good, but I certainly wouldn't send the summary to my readers. It's a step along the road, rather than a final destination.

### Summarising research

I paste the work of others to find key words and interesting themes. This is about 40% successful. I find it tends to ignore opposing views and rebuttals, so it often produces one-sided summaries which don't reflect the complexity of an issue.

When I'm not sure if a research paper is worth diving into, I put in TL;DR (too long, didn't read) into the app. My AI helper will give me a brief summary which helps me decide if an article is worthy of further investigation.

### Analysing a writer's tone of voice

This is fun. Put in some text and then ask AI to *analyse my writing style*. This is great for identifying mismatches between the voice you want (formal, authoritative) and what you've actually written (informal, light-hearted).

I put some text from Margate Bookie into the mixer. ChatGPT is very positive – *you are a clear writer who handles the material well* – but details are lacking. I use it when team members write blog posts. It's a quick way to see if they establish the tone I'm looking for (friendly rather than austere, supportive without being patronising) but it's no substitute for a proper edit.

Lap 16, by the way, and I'm blowing hard.

### Rewriting it as someone else

AI is the great mimic, and it can (sort of) reimagine your writing in the style of, say, Naguib Mahfouz or Isabel Allende. Here's the opening of this chapter as if written by the fourteenth-century poet Geoffry Chaucer.

*Whan January, with its chilly hand of fate,*
*Hath brought us to the brink of manuscript's end,*
*And in its wake, a lingering concern doth wait,*
*For in this chapter, technology doth bend.*

Fun, but unlikely to be much help with that RFP.

### Turning my book into a musical

I'm kidding.

### Producing original content

I'm also kidding.

I'm out of breath now, and my goggles are getting a bit tight. (I blame this on the design of my nose, rather than the design of the goggles.)

My slightly breathless conclusion? Treat AI as a tool or a toy, but don't rely on it to do the job of a writer. It's not good enough for that, and you're better than that as well. I do encourage you to play with the apps, but AI doesn't have a heart or a soul and it's definitely not creative. It remixes what's out there but doesn't produce anything original. In the words of comedy writing guru Paul Dornan, 'AI gives you more but it won't give you new.'

## Where to now

Chapter 10 – a unique brand voice cannot (yet) be created by AI. It's too specialised, too idiosyncratic. If you need persuading, go back to our chapter on Finding Your Voice.

Chapter 18 – can AI beat the humans at summarising? I'm not sure, but I reckon it's worth trying when you write your first draft. Just make sure you use it as a tool to help you, rather than a replacement for your own hard work.

Try this. I think of myself as open-minded, and I'm the sort of person who's always searching for time-saving hacks. I just don't think AI technologies are right for writing. If you think you can convince me otherwise, do send me a message. I'll leave it to you whether you use ChatGPT or not.

# Part 5

# Polishing

## Making the Diamond Shine

# Chapter 17

# The essential polishes – editing, revising, proofing

### The Penis mightier than the sword

Yes, dear reader, I did once put that at the end of an email. As I was to find to my cost, spellcheck doesn't pick up this type of error.

*Submission tension* is the unease we feel before we send the RFP to our biggest client or email the report to the 500 people on our distribution list. Submission tension makes us anxious at the very moment we would most benefit from suggestions for improvement. Instead of being receptive to ideas, we clam up.

How do you reduce submission tension? First up, ask for feedback. Then edit and proof, preferably with the help of other people. Many people have the mistaken belief that writing is a solitary process, but the best writers always ask for second opinions.

I'm going to talk about the three different stages that exist between you finishing your draft version and you pressing send. In an ideal world you have time to rest and relax between each stage. But we don't live in an ideal world, so the boundaries between these stages are often blurred.

*Figure 17.1*

DOI: 10.4324/9781003513520-22

### Stage 1 – feedback

I'm still watching the Beatles documentary, *Get Back*. I'm somewhere in the seventh hour. Macca's playing a couple of bum notes on the piano, John's on out-of-time drums, Ringo looks a bit stoned. They want George to add some lead but the hands of the guitar god are fully occupied with buttering a couple of slices of toast. It's a mess, but that afternoon the flubs and botches turn into *The Long and Winding Road*. Creating anything of worth is often a messy job.

Many of us have painful memories of getting our work reviewed. The teacher who complained about your handwriting when you were eight, or that exam you flunked when you were sixteen. All of us have had homework come back covered in red ink, with a frightening *SEE ME* in block capitals at the bottom of the page. We fear the same is going to happen at work.

The document you're working on is only a first draft, and first drafts are usually clogged up with mistakes. No matter how hard you've worked, and how much love you've spent, you're still in rehearsals. The finished album and the rooftop gig are close but still not close enough.

### Get feedback, and get it early

Responding to feedback will always improve your work. A relatively small amount of pain leads to big gains and the satisfying feeling that your work is getting better.

The best time to get valuable feedback is after your first or second draft. Before this point, your ideas will still be in a state of flux and you'll be too easily swayed by the opinions of others. After this point, you may well be too set in your ideas and approach to appreciate input from others.

### The three P's of feedback

Remind yourself of these thoughts if you are resistant to feedback.

*Keep your perspective.* Adding the odd comma[1] or deleting a clunky sentence isn't an insult to your genius. Most of your work is still good. Loads of improvements can be made quickly and without too much effort. These tweaks immediately improve your work, but you can only make them because a second pair of eyes has checked it.

*Feedback isn't personal.* People aren't attacking you if they suggest a paragraph is moved to another section. You'd tell your colleague if they had gravy stains on their shirt or were flying low after a visit to the bathroom, wouldn't you? They're doing the same with their feedback. They're actually stopping you from making mistakes in public, and for that you should be grateful.

*Remain positive.* Smart feedback improves the piece you're finishing, and great feedback improves you as a writer. It's worth it. Constructive criticism transforms the good enough into something wonderful.

You need to give yourself time to respond to feedback. A big tip is to check the new changes you make to your drafts very carefully. For a number of reasons – tiredness, over-familiarity, resistance to the comments of others – you might find yourself actually increasing the number of typos rather than reducing them.

### Stage 2 – editing

You're up against it. The internet spews out over 40 billion quadrillion words every second on new sites, blogs, ads and tweets.[2] We live in a time where everyone with a computer can publish. The problem is that, sadly, not everyone with a computer can write.

There are two reasons why business writers press send too early.

1. Positive – you're desperate to share your writing with the whole world. How can people live without your burning prose and trenchant analysis?
2. Negative – you're eager to put a big fat tick next to a big fat item on your To Do list. Will this damned project never end?

To be a writer of influence you need to shift away from both these limiting mindsets. The extra 5% of reviewing effort tightens up your word choice, sentence construction and order of paragraphs. By focusing on the readers' needs, rather than on the deadline that's speeding towards you like a torpedo, you'll gain loyal readers.

Readers may forgive the occasional typo, but too many errors are bad for your image. You'll come across as sloppy and uncaring, even as untrustworthy. Don't ruin your company's reputation by sending out a rubbish draft. Editing is fiddly and demands patience, but it's vital. As an absolute minimum, use the Editor in Word (although be wary of its rather odd grammar suggestions).

Editing is when we can reduce our word count or add signposts to make our argument clearer. Don't force your reader to hack through your writing with a machete to find your message. These tune-ups are especially important in the beginning of your piece – only a fool spends more time on the appendix than the headline.

It's a fine balance because you are the expert in readers' eyes. Resist the urge to delete explanations and examples because you fear they may be too simple. Most of your readers will be beginners in the subject, not experts. It's a bit like an exam at school. Whilst it's great to show off your higher learning, makes sure you score the easy marks by covering the basics.

*Stage 3 – proofing*

The fat lady isn't yet singing, but she's definitely doing her warm-ups. Proofing is your last chance to spot mistakes before you press send. Scanning over a printout should highlight poor design and silly mistakes like numbered lists that start at 2.1 and end at xvi. Check high-risk areas – the names of people and countries, whether a currency is yen or euros – even if you're in the 59th minute of the eleventh hour.

## Read it aloud

Reading out loud is the best method to highlight sentences and words that need improvement. Do it every time you edit your work, because it will always make it better. This used to be harder when we worked in offices and had to pretend to be on a conference call so we could shut the door behind us. Now that most of us spend more time at home, looking stupid isn't such a concern.

Listen to your voice. It'll give you these following clues.

*Stumbles.* The sentence needs to be reworked because there's something clunky about the grammar or the words. If your polysyllabic turpitude gets you tongue-tied, then it'll be even harder for someone else to read.

*Fade Outs.* If you notice your voice dropping off towards the end of a section, you've probably written too much. Consider cutting sections or changing the structure, and be aware of paragraphs where you repeat ideas.

*Gulps.* If you're out of breath, your sentences are too long, usually because you've got clause build-up. (Flip back to Chapter 7 for an explanation of clauses.) You can play around with punctuation, but it's invariably better for you and your reader to split a big chunk of text into shorter sentences.

*Rat-a-tat.* Listen out for the chop-chop-chop of too many short sentences close to each other. Rework them.

*CBA.* If you can't be bothered to read out a section, delete it. Your reader won't notice the missing text.

## What is cognitive cost, and why should you reduce it?

I've worked with some really clever people – and some right idiots as well. Joanne Beresford edited research at a bank. I asked her if she could reduce an eight-page report on a company's share price to a single page. Her approach was to reduce the font size from 14 pt to 6 pt, delete all the headings and subheadings and turn off the borders in Word so she could print right to the edges of the A4. *Cognitive cost* made it unreadable.

Cognitive cost is shorthand for anything that gets between your reader and your writing. The problems could be at their end (they're distracted by colleagues, they've lost their glasses) but usually it's down to us. We've made the text too small, we've printed yellow text on a purple background, we're writing ten-line sentences in landscape format. Cognitive cost sucks up a reader's processing power, and that will turn them against you

## Proofing is your final polish

Duncan, who I met when I worked at Oxford University Press, is a professional proofer. He's responsible for signing off books at a big publisher in London, so his attention to detail veers towards the obsessive.

'Hello. You seem to have put on a couple of kilos', is his greeting. (See what I mean about his attention to detail?) We sit outside Bar Italia, and I pull in my tummy as Duncan gives me his top editing tips.

'Before I do anything, I email myself a copy of the most recent version. My computer saves to so many drives – Google, Prime, Dropbox – that I want to make sure I can find the author's original in case I screw up. It's comforting to have the original version safe and sound in Cyberspace'.

'Good point. What else?'

'Put your focus on the high-risk areas. Check headlines, place names and numbers. And double check people's names, because people are super-sensitive about being misspelled. This applies as much to simple names – are they Jon or John? – as much as it does to linguistic nightmares like Loizou'.

'Ta. Another coffee?'

'Sure. But I'll eat the amaretto biscuit for you'.

'How kind. Next tip?'

'Over the years I've noticed that mistakes tend to appear in clusters. It's because the writer was tired or distracted or was wrestling with complex material. If you find two errors close to each other, you'll find more lurking close by'.

'Fair point. What else?'

'Proofing hurts the eyes. I recommend people take a break every thirty minutes to rest and refocus. If you're proofing your own work, you must leave some time between finishing the edit and proofing. You're using a different part of your brain to do different jobs'.

'Have you got a snappy image for this change in mindset I could use in my book?'

'Hmmm'. He stares at me across the table. 'You have to deliberately strip off your editor's cardigan before putting on your proofer's hat'.

'Hmmm', I reply, 'I'll use that if can't think of anything better'.

And if you can't think of anything better at this stage, you might just be ready to press send.

Good luck!

## Where to now?

Chapter 2 – I like to remind myself of my original objectives before I enter the revising and polishing stage. Check *why* you're writing. This is a good time to delete sentences and paragraphs that don't add to your argument.

Chapter 14 – do you remember what we learned about processing speeds when reading? Editing is your last chance to boost the clarity of your writing, so do it with focus and attention.

Be aware of your reaction when you encounter sloppy sentences, lackadaisical grammar and stupid spelling mistakes. Notice how they weaken your respect for the writer. Don't be them.

## Notes

1 In an art-imitating-life moment, my editor noticed that I'd used the phrase *the odd coma* in my draft manuscript.
2 I've obviously made up this statistic; just everyone else does with statistics on the internet. The thing to remember is that you face a lot of competition.

# Chapter 18

# Summaries and info tables

We live in a world of reduction. Everyone wants their information quicker and no-one has time to read everything. People ask for a summary – *just the facts, Ma'am* – many more times than they ask you for longer explanations or deeper details.

A summary expresses the main ideas of an article or a report. The emphasis is on speed, so the summary has to be much shorter than the original. I tend to aim for 25% to begin with. In the case of an executive summary, which appears on the report's cover, I'm looking at 1% of the original.

I'm going to teach you two ways to produce great summaries. The first, called read/reduce/rewrite, is the more traditional and the easiest to do. The second, info tables, is easier for the reader but demands more work from you. Along the way, I'll also prove to you why bullet points are crap.

This method works equally well if you're summarising your own work or the work of someone else. But please understand there's always a trade-off. To save the reader's time, you need to lose details and cut examples. And maybe you'll lose a little politeness as well. Your readers will forgive these sacrifices because you're saving their valuable time.

## Read

Read the whole text first. Don't be tempted to write a summary *before* you understand the main ideas. Without sounding like Captain Obvious (one of Marvel's less popular super-heroes), you need to know the size and content of the original before you can summarise.

An initial scan will help you. The contents page and chapter titles should tell you the main ideas. If the original is written and designed with care, you should get the gist by looking at headers and topic sentences.[1] Highlight or underline main points and key phrases, and then divide the text into grouped ideas. Your job is to select the major points, knowing that you can't cover everything.

DOI: 10.4324/9781003513520-23

The Read/Reduce/Rewrite method

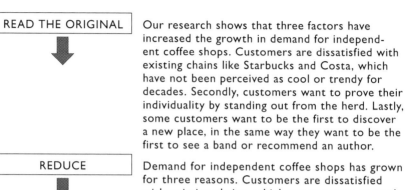

**READ THE ORIGINAL**

Our research shows that three factors have increased the growth in demand for independent coffee shops. Customers are dissatisfied with existing chains like Starbucks and Costa, which have not been perceived as cool or trendy for decades. Secondly, customers want to prove their individuality by standing out from the herd. Lastly, some customers want to be the first to discover a new place, in the same way they want to be the first to see a band or recommend an author.

**REDUCE**

Demand for independent coffee shops has grown for three reasons. Customers are dissatisfied with existing chains, which are not seen as cool. Customers want to stand out from the herd to prove their individuality. Customers want to be the first to discover a new place, like a new band or author

**REWRITE**

Independent coffee shops are more popular:
1 Existing chains are seen as uncool.
2 Customers want to show they are individuals.
3 Customers want to be the first to find a new place.

(I reckon 2 and 3 could be combined.)

## Reduce

I usually switch to a printout. I love crossing out chunks of data or screeds of examples that I don't need.

You need to be objective when you reduce. If the original contains three reasons why your start-up should launch digital paperweights, and two reasons why it shouldn't, you need to include the pros *and* the cons. If you include only one side of the argument, you're not producing a fair summary. Instead, you're producing your own version based on your biases and personal interests. And that's when the writer of the original tends to get really annoyed.

You'll be guided by two constraints: how few words you're allowed for the summary, and how little time you have to write them. You need to decide what are the essential points and what's peripheral. And this will lead you to consider the level of detail you can present.

## Rewrite

Now you need to write a short sentence for each point. If these are torturous, full of *ifs* and *buts* and multiple clauses, you haven't reduced enough. But when you've got these lines ready, combine them into a first draft. Make sure it flows well, in a logical order. Ctrl/C and Ctrl/V are your best friends here.

## Tips for rewriting

1. No evidence, no examples

> A controversial point, but summaries don't contain statistics, numbers or quotes from interviews. These all back up the writer's main points, but they're not main points in themselves.
>
> (I'm not dogmatic here. If there's a really telling fact or a revealing statistic, bung it in. But be conscious of the trade-off because you've added a sentence.)

2. Their ideas, your words

> I recommend that you use your own words for the summary. You can make life a lot easier for the reader by swapping business phrases (*top line revenues*, *break down the silos*) for their everyday, human equivalents (*sales, sharing info*). Shorter words and punchier sentences increase readability, and that's essential for a top quality summary.

3. Polish, proof

> Just like any other piece of writing, don't rush and send it out unchecked. You're putting your name to this, so proof read, check spelling and spend effort on the formatting. If you've done your job well, you won't need tons of time. If there's time, ask for – and use – feedback.

4. Check the meaning

> Return to the original and make sure you're truly representing the author's intentions. Is there anything vital that you've missed? You have a 'duty of care' towards the original writer, and so you must reflect their viewpoint. And that writer could be you.
>
> You'll know your summary has hit the mark when the reader doesn't need to read the original. You've created something new, a piece of writing that stands on its own legs. Like all good writing, it's clear and coherent and tells the reader what they want to know.

## Why do we all hate bullet points?

Bullet points are the lowest form of communication available to Mankind. They first appeared in the early 1980s, like stonewashed jeans and *Flashdance*, and their impact has been just as disastrous. What started as a way to break up solid blocks of text on flipcharts and overhead projectors soon became a curse. Lazy writers pretend they're a replacement for summaries, but no-one believes them.

We all know we're cheating when we produce bullet points. Some of us may spend time tinkering with the odd word, or even changing the round bullet point into a square or – gasp – an arrow. But we never lose that nagging feeling that bullet pointed lists don't work.

## Why not? They are

- Boring to look at
- Overused and overused and repetitive and repetitive
- Often miss out something that's important to us
- Subject to formatting errors because the writer doesn't check them
- Usually just a chunk of dull text that someone has pasted from the main document and figured out how to add in Word
- Disorganised, just jumbled together into a list

Hands up if you skipped this list? Most of you, which is just what I expected. Your eye may have scanned the words, but the words forged no connection with your brain. By the time you've got to the end of this chapter, you'll not only have forgotten what's on this list, you'll probably even have forgotten that there was a list.

The next time you're yawning through a screen of random bullets, consider the impression the writer makes on you. They may be the great expert on their subject, but their sloppy way of presenting does them no favours. They're dumping data on you because they believe bullets are a quick way to communicate, but we feel that they don't care about the reader. They've used bullets because any old fool can copy and paste them from the main text. And, with a gulp of shame, we realise that we're as guilty as them.

C'mon people, there must be a better way than this.

## Info tables are the solution

Info tables are more work for you, but they have one hundred times the impact. Think of them as a beautifully constructed bridge between your content and your reader.

Allow me to explain. An info table is two to four columns wide and three to five rows deep. There's space at the top to write your most important message. The tight format forces you to organise your thoughts into binaries – *good v bad, this year v next year, North v South, risky v safe* – which helps your reader grasp the main points. Because there's a limit on the number of items you can cover, you can only cover the most important points. And that is what makes info tables great for summaries.

**Buy Empatica (1)**

| Impact on Income Statement (3) | Without Empatica | With Empatica (2) |
|---|---|---|
| Revenue (4) | Market share declining (5)<br><br>*Stagnation of sales since COVID* | Expanding Asian markets<br><br>*Access to new markets and cross-selling. Forecast of 8% YoY* |
| Gross margin (4) | Falling<br><br>*High competition causes low margin (2.4%) (6)* | Growing<br><br>*Launch in new markets will offer high margin opportunities (7.5%)* |

An example will help. Imagine I'm reporting to you about taking over a consulting firm. I start off by stating my conclusion very clearly and at the point of maximum prominence. *Buy Empatica (1).*

On the top, horizontal line of the table I show the two scenarios I'm considering. I immediately set up the distinction between *Without Empatica* and *With Empatica (2).* Segmenting my findings into these *category pairs*[2] makes it easy for readers to follow my thoughts. Note how the lack of space forces me to choose short words.

I make it clear that we're looking at a specific area of the company's operations – *Impact on Income Statement (3).* Instead of covering every possible factor, I chose the two that will have the most material impact on the company's income - Revenue and Gross margin *(4).*

Next I fill in the table. I know people skim, so each box gets a phrase that I limit to a maximum of three words *(5).* Again, the constrictions imposed by the design force me to think harder and reduce more. Sometimes a single world – *falling, growing* – is enough.

Below each bullet point I add some brief details, adding examples and explanations for readers who want more depth *(6).* The details I advised you to cut out of the read/reduce/rewrite summary look good in an info table. See how the italics make it look distinct from the main point, as if to say *this is interesting but optional.*

Why do info tables score over bullet points? First up, the writer has to work harder and that's always beneficial for readers. The random splattering of bullets is replaced by structure and organisation. White spaces and typography make it look more attractive. If you forget something, a blank space will remind you that work is still needed. And you communicate to your reader that you care about their time, that you are in control of your material, and yes, it is a good moment to talk about that raise now.

Hold on. Why don't I summarise all these advantages in an info table?

### Use info tables

| Why Info Tables Rule | Info Tables | Bullet Points |
|---|---|---|
| Easier to read | Organised | Disorganised |
| Increase writer's authority | Control over the material | Looks sloppy |
| Less words<br><br>Shows completeness | Quicker to read<br><br>Obvious if something missing | Cut and paste<br><br>Can't tell if something is missing |

### If you have to use bullet points . . .

By now, my hatred of bullets should be well established. But, if you feel that you must use them, front loading makes them less painful.

Look for what applies to all your points, and then only have what's different in the bullets. Here's the bad example, where words are unnecessarily repeated:

#### Buy this book

- because you want to learn about business writing
- because you want to learn about readers' needs
- because you want to learn about style and voice

The good example front-loads the words that apply to all three points.

#### Buy this book because you want to learn about

- business writing
- readers' needs
- style and voice

You've cut down 28 words to 16, without any loss in meaning. And you've made it far easier for the reader to see the reasons why they should buy the book.

## Where to now?

Chapter 8 your bullet points need precise, punchy words. Circumventing Latinate lexicography will ameliorate your slides. And will take up less space.

Chapter 13 – by now you'll have realised that I regard bullet points as the antithesis of charismatic writing. Remind yourself how carefully selected words create the connection that lists never can.

Look out for good examples of how info tables present lots of information quickly and with clarity. Look out for bad examples of how bullet points are used by lazy writers. Choose your weapons wisely.

## Notes

1 We covered topic sentences in Chapter 6. To remind you, a topic sentence is the first sentence in a paragraph.
2 I know, jargon term, guilty as charged.

# Chapter 19

# Design and visuals

## No-one is more predictable than a reader with a choice

There you are, sprawled on the sofa after another tough day. You're doom-scrolling on your phone because you're too tired to watch Netflix, yet too wired to go to sleep. You find two articles with exactly the same head-line: *here's seven things you don't known about clickbait.* They seem to be about the same length, the same quality and the same readability. How do you choose your next dopamine buzz?

The look.

Does the author profile pic scream *I've cut this from a wedding photo that's nine years old?* Are there/they're/their grammar mistakes, repeated words and spelling howlers in the intro? Is it all yellow text on a pink background, flashing banners, in a font that's too small to read or too big to fit on your screen?

The look means you click on the article which has the most attractive design.

Exactly the same process is in play when you're faced with two reports with similar content. The well-designed document gets more readers than the random brain dump. We're always told not to judge a book by its cover. But we all do.

## Two ways to make great first impressions

### 1. Start at the end

Get your conclusion on the front page. This is your recommendation, your finding, the one idea your reader has to know.

This isn't the time to indulge your inner scriptwriter. You're the exact opposite of a storyteller, who wants to build up the tension with twist after twist until a surprise revelation in the last scene.

DOI: 10.4324/9781003513520-24

And if you're telling someone about *Titanic*, the message you need to highlight is that the big ship sinks at the end.

### 2. Consider the flickers

Readers of physical documents take one last step before they decide. They'll flick through, even if just for a second, to confirm their interest.

*People who flick from the front.* They're searching for structure, so keep them happy with a contents page, organised modules, chapter titles, headlines and subheadings.

*People who flick from the back.* They're more interested in the look and feel of the report. Make sure you've got lots of white space, some great pictures and a reasonable font size. And for the love of God, don't include an appendix because that's Latin for *no-one will ever read this*.

One thing you often see with printed work is people balancing the document or book in the palm of their hand. They're literally weighing up the effort they're going to need. If your report is particularly 'heavy', make sure that your design gives it some lightness.

### The just noticeable difference

Let's take a quick detour into psychophysics. The theory of the Just Noticeable Difference (JND) explains how our brains perceive an external stimulus. JND informs decisions as different as the safe decibel level on your phone and how far the manufacturers can shrink Toblerones before we notice. JND isn't some abstruse and arcane academic backwater. Its impact is everywhere, and it leads to one design rule that always works for business writers.

So, Professor Loizou, what's the implication for report design? The JND measures the smallest change in your formatting that your customers or audience will notice. The JND in writing design is much smaller than you think. All you need to do is put a word in **bold** or *italics*, and your eye will tell your brain something different is happening. CAPITALISATION and the slightest change in font (size or type) will be noticed.

So keep your formatting changes really simple and trust your reader to notice. One difference is all that is needed. Our eyes become exhausted when designers *add* **too MANY CHANGES**. Exhausted readers don't stick around to get even more tired.

### Two easy wins for designing tables

I want to give you two tips that will make the graphs in your report absolutely swing. It's time to wave goodbye to those doughnut-skewed pie charts that make zero sense.[1]

## Nothing easier – or better – than an infographic

I wrote a report to show funders that people were travelling from abroad to attend the Margate Bookie. My first thought was to present the results of our survey as a traditional Excel chart. After wasting 20 minutes of my precious life, I came up with this:

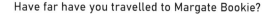

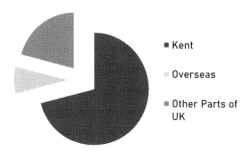

*Figure 19.1*

What's wrong with this picture? Your eye is automatically drawn to the biggest slice (*Kent*) but I actually want to talk about the smallest chunk (*overseas*), which kind of becomes invisible in the pie chart. The three other chunks (*Kent, London, Other Parts of the UK*) are irrelevant and distracting. And because I was stressed and against the clock, I forgot how to put percentages next to the important chunk. I could, of course, have gone to YouTube and searched for a How To video, but, come on, who has time for that?

An infographic solved these problems in a way that it as simple as it is obvious:

**8%**
of our visitors
   travelled from
   abroad

Why is this a winner? People can find the most important point without having to decipher the graph and divine my meaning. I did the graphic in less than a minute, so plenty of my time was saved as well. And next year, I'm looking at two seconds of work to show how the number has changed.

## Comparison tables

This is a smart technique to communicate your findings as quickly as possible. I teach a group of corporate lawyers in Luxembourg whose ultimate client, Regine, buys and (very successfully) sells fintechs that have been running for between three and five years.

Regine's very much got *the vision thing*. She pays the lawyers to do research and due diligence, but there's no way she'll ever read their thick reports, full of legal arcana like *the afore-mentioned intellectual property* and *pacta sunt servanda*. She wants them to do the work, but she doesn't want to see their workings.

So I worked with the lawyers to come up with a comparison table that always appears on the second page of their report. (The first page lists their recommendation, which they tend to be a little scared to give.)

Let's say Regine is considering three different companies. (I can't give you the names, so I'm using stand-ins from the prehistoric era of the World Wide Web.) Regine evaluates the possible investments using just four criteria, which are listed on the first column on the left.

The marking scheme is simplicity itself. A tick means good, a cross means bad. (On occasions, the lawyers get excited and use a double tick for a company, which is exceptionally good, but this is Luxembourg so such craziness doesn't happen too often.) The result – Alta Vista looks the best choice – jumps out. They put this in bold to make it clear. JND has done its job.

|  | Ask Jeeves | Alta Vista | AOL |
|---|---|---|---|
| Debt to Equity ratio below 1.0 | x | ✔ | x |
| Top Three market position in five major markets | ✔ | ✔ | ✔ |
| Growth of Turnover over last 3 years above 25% CAGR | ✔ | ✔ | x |
| Female to Male representation on board above 60% | x | x | ✔ |

This format makes it easy for Regine to compare the three companies. She describes it as 'like running my finger down a menu'. Regine is happy that the lawyers stick to only four evaluation criteria. Slightly torturing the restaurant analogy, she tells me that the lack of too many options makes ordering much quicker. The lawyers keep the evaluation criteria consistent, so Regine will see exactly the same approach when she next commissions a report.

The design limits the number of words the lawyers can use, which is always a good thing. On the rare occasions when the lawyers are still working on an answer or don't have enough information, they leave the cell blank so Regine immediately knows that it's still work-in-progress. And it's very easy to link from this summary table to the relevant chapter or module if Regine wants more detail to help her make her decision. (She never does, but it's still good to have.)

### Where to now?

We're nearly at the end of the book, so I'm going to change tack. Many of us have a writer or a magazine we like. Go back to them and work out how they managed to influence you.

You'll find that the best writers shows simultaneously all the attributes of *Write Now!* They have a unique personal voice, they tell stories, their style is clear and concise and human. Their arguments are logically ordered. They plan and polish. Above all, they write with the reader in mind.

The phrase *talent borrows but genius steals* is an encouragement not a warning. Copy people you like until your own talent shines through.

### Note

1 Financial people and scientists – you've spent your whole life interpreting graphs. Finding the median point on a box and whisker graph of t-stats is a piece of cake. However, the sculptors and poets amongst your audience may expend considerable cognitive cost every time they see a graph. Keep this in mind.

# Chapter 20

# What is readability, and how do you get it?

No-one will ever ask you to make your sentences longer. No-one wants your writing to be twice as complicated or three times as convoluted. A reader may ask you for more detail or a deeper explanation, but she'll never say *it'll be great if you could make your writing absolutely impenetrable.*

What she wants is readability. This is the word that captures all those objectives we talked about way back in Chapter 1. She wants the text in front of her to be clear, concise, precise, interesting, fresh and human. No matter how great your content, if your style stinks, she's going to ditch you.

You know this from your own experiences of reading vague and dull white papers. You blame yourself the first time you have to re-read a sentence because you lost focus. The second time you blame the writer. And the third time, you stop reading. You now believe the writer is sloppy and a poor communicator. Even worse, you begin to doubt if they really understand their subject.

Being easily understood is vital, especially when readers have so many alternatives begging for their attention. We're all busy, and none of us wants to waste our precious time on poor writing, which leads us to the elusive quality of readability. I want to be positive in this chapter, so I'll give you examples from all round the world that show great readability. But first, some stats.

## What determines readability?

There are two main factors – sentence length and word choice.

The relationship between writing long sentences and losing your readers is clear. If your average sentence length is 25 words, a third of your readers will probably get confused or take the wrong meaning or feel lost. (The sentence you just read contained 25 words.) Go longer than that, and many of your readers will need to re-read, even if they are mega-interested in your topic.

DOI: 10.4324/9781003513520-25

| Word Count | Reader Response | Readers Lost |
|:---:|:---|:---:|
| 8 | It's easy | 0% |
| 15 | It's OK | 10% |
| 20 | It's tough | 25% |
| 25 | I'm not wasting my time and effort on this trash | 35% |

It's a myth that a complex topic must lead to dense writing. The opposite should be true. It's your job to explain a technically challenging topic in a way that your audience can understand. The narcotic combination of long sentences and very technical terms is definitely something to be avoided.

## Four instant ways to make your sentences punchier

1. Stick to one idea per sentence. This stops you from piling up lots of embedded clauses, those half sentences marked out by commas, which can clog up your writing. Delete them if they add nothing, or turn them into sentences in their own right.
2. Cut your adverbs. I'm a big fan of adjectives (words which describe a thing or person in more detail) but have little time for adverbs (words which describe how an action is done). For me, they're a sign of imprecise language. Far better to write *Kaylan guzzled her food* rather than *Kaylan ate her food quickly*. Readers will appreciate the extra work you put in to find the right verb.
3. Imagine your reader is a student and you are a teacher. Picture a learner between 16 and 19, someone who's in the last years of secondary school or just starting university. They're not at a genius level, but they're clever. You'll keep them away for TikTok by writing sentences between 10 and 20 words and keeping your paragraphs to four sentences max.
4. Take a tip from the crime writers. When you read a police interrogation scene, the fast-paced dialogue perks you up. Why? The lines are snappier; there's more conflict and more action. Your eyes zoom through the white space. Make the same happen with your business writing. Use short lines to give momentum. Readers love the sensation of making progress through a document.

## Sometimes readability comes from adding, not taking away

Time for a switcheroo. Over the last 19 chapters, I've talked often about the need to cut down your writing. My advice has always been about reduction – delete verbiage to make your message clear, choose short words over long words, split a ten-line sentence into three easier sentences.

But now, just for a page and a half, I want you to ignore my previous suggestions and think about how you can improve your message by adding text. Surprised? Read on for three ways more can be more.

### 1. Add an expert

This is a great technique when you feel your credibility needs a boost. Your opinions and insights into your business are valuable, but to reach a bigger audience, you need to work your contacts. Is there an expert or authority who can add some wisdom to your blog? Sprinkle some quotes from them in your blog post, and you'll benefit from the association.

Make sure the quotes are relevant to the reader. And don't just rehash comments that are already clogging up the internet. We've already got too many amateurs doing that.

### 2. Compile your greatest hits

Lots of small business owners build loyalty with regular posts about, say, their favourite recipes or their most effective exercise problems. But new customers need to dedicate time to scrolling through possibly hundreds of posts before finding your key message.

Help them out. Curate your ten best posts into *A Beginner's Guide to Fundraising* or *Ten Tips to Make You a Better Boss*. Put your most important info in a single place so it's easy to find. Your care and organisation will turn new visitors into loyal customers.

### 3. Get your retaliation in first

Remember rebuttals in Chapter 12? This was a deliberate ploy by a writer to highlight criticism of their ideas. It makes a writer seem more truthful and open-minded, which creates trust and rapport with the reader.

One of my favourite novels of all time is *The Wasp Factory* by the Scottish writer Iain Banks. I warn you that it's a read that divides opinion. The literary critic of *The Irish Times*, for example, didn't mince their words. 'It's a sick, sick world when the confidence and investment of an astute firm of publishers is justified by a work of unparalleled depravity'. *The Sunday Express* called it 'a silly, gloatingly sadistic and grisly yarn', and *The Times* dismissed it succinctly as 'rubbish'.

But the publishers came up with a masterstroke. They interspersed negative reviews amongst all the positive reactions the book received, and printed them on the inside front pages. This move alerted readers that the book wasn't for everyone. And it also created a sense of us against them, the brave reader against the fuddy-duddy literary establishment. For a book about finding your identity, this was a very canny strategy.

This is, for sure, a high-risk strategy. But it pays off for companies who want to be seen as truthful and empathetic.

It's been quite a while since I set you an exercise. Let me right this wrong with these six sentences I collected over the last two days, while at a conference of such mind-blasting tedium that I've already forgotten what it was called or where it was held. But these six terrible sentences have stuck with me.

1. We can *ameliorate* the shortfall *by means of* regular cashflow payments.
2. *It is compulsory for you* to sign the contract.
3. The *optimum* way to meet VC contacts is *by means of* preparation.
4. *Despite the fact that* the service is expensive, I *am of the opinion that* it is worth buying.
5. It is *erroneous* to *intimate* that insurance is cheap, *notwithstanding* our contacts in the industry.
6. We better understood the client's *requirements, subsequent to* the second meeting.

You job is to change the italicised words in these sentences to make them easier to read. Here are the words I suggest you use: after, although, best, by, despite, even if, mostly, reduce say, think, needs, while, with, wrong, you must.

## Suggested answers

I don't mind if you've chosen other words, as long as they are short. Anything that helps readability is great, even if we disagree on the exact word!

1. We can *reduce* the shortfall *with* regular cashflow payments.
2. *You must* sign the contract.
3. The *best* way to impress VC contacts is *by* preparation.
4. *Even if* the service is expensive, I *think* it is worth buying.
5. It is *wrong* to *say* that insurance is cheap, *despite* our contacts in the industry.
6. We better understood the client's *needs, after* the second meeting.

## Where to now?

Follow me on LinkedIn and AndreasLearning.com. You know you want to.
   Read. Find examples of great writing and work out why it changed you.
   Genius steals. Copy the style of a business writer you admire.
   Until we next meet . . .

# Index

Printed in the United States
by Baker & Taylor Publisher Services